GRILLING

280+ SIZZLING RECIPES
— FOR YEAR-ROUND GRILLING —

GRILLING

13-Digit ISBN: 978-1-60433-730-3
10-Digit ISBN: 1-60433-730-3

This book may be ordered by mail from the publisher. Please include $5.99 for postage and handling
Please support your local bookseller first!

Books published by Cider Mill Press Book Publishers are available at special discounts for bulk purchases in the United States by corporations, institutions, and other organizations. For more information, please contact the publisher.

Cider Mill Press Book Publishers
"Where good books are ready for press"
PO Box 454
12 Spring Street
Kennebunkport, Maine 04046
Visit us online!
www.cidermillpress.com

Typography: Acumin Pro, Minion Pro, Knockout
Image Credits: Photograph on page 359 courtesy of Derek Bissonnette.
All other images used under official license from Shutterstock.com.

Printed in China

1 2 3 4 5 6 7 8 9 0

First Edition

GRILLING

280+ SIZZLING RECIPES
— FOR YEAR-ROUND GRILLING —

JOHN WHALEN III

CIDER MILL PRESS

BOOK PUBLISHERS

KENNEBUNKPORT, MAINE

CONTENTS

INTRODUCTION

THE ART OF THE FLAME

At the most fundamental level, grilling is the ability to understand and work with fire. Learning how to build, maintain, and control the fire when cooking meats and vegetables is essential to grilling. Contrary to popular belief, grilling is not simply owning the fanciest grill on the market; rather, it is the ability to build a fire and cook over it. Whether you are using a gas or charcoal grill, or a firepit in your backyard, grilling is all about your ability to master the art of the flame.

Whether you are just starting out on your grilling adventure, or you have been around the block a few times and know the ins and outs of grilling and barbecue, you can always learn more. A trip down to backcountry Texas for the local barbecue will surely show you just how far you have to go. It was on a Texas road trip that I truly began to learn the subtle differences in barbecuing techniques and recipes in the local towns; while some held the philosophy that a good barbecue is all in the sauce, others focused on the rubs and marinades, followed by the slow grilling of meats. Another trip, to Chongqing, China, exposed me to an entirely new sort of grilling. Here, BBQ begins around nightfall and runs all the way until sunrise. The dishes are spicy and dry—not sugary—making for a perfect late-night snack.

Whether you're in North Carolina, Maine, or even in China, mastering the art of the flame is essential to grilling. For anyone who is just starting their grilling adventures, true, flavor-packed grilling begins with learning how to use flame to bring out the best in any preparation.

TYPES OF GRILLS

The word "grill" brings to mind the stereotypical backyard American grill, but grills come in many forms all over the world. In China, their version of the "grill" is a small fire built on the sidewalk using wood or small coals and topped with a makeshift grate. It is similar to the Japanese konro, which is used for yakitori—a delicious meal of skewered and grilled meats. By focusing on the fire, we can get a better idea of the various styles of grills.

CHARCOAL GRILL

If I had to recommend one type of grill to someone just starting out, this is it. The fire from a charcoal grill comes from the pit of charcoal briquettes that you light and stoke while grilling. Charcoal grills are relatively inexpensive (I highly recommend the manufacturer Weber), and the smoke from the charcoal adds a great taste to meats and vegetables. Charcoal grills require more work to start than gas or portable grills—the charcoal briquettes take longer to heat, and you often need to use charcoal chimneys in order to light in the beginning—but that extra work is very instructive as you begin to master the art of the flame!

GAS GRILL

When you think of modern grilling, you probably think of the large, stainless-steel gas grill set on the back patio. Gas grills are much more expensive than charcoal and portable grills, but the investment goes a long way. Gas grills are easier to understand, convenient to cook on, and require a lot less cleanup than a charcoal grill. For all their beauty and ease, gas grills do not offer the same level of control over the flame as charcoal or open-fire grills.

PORTABLE GRILL

These grills come in both countertop and standing forms and are perfect for camping, indoor cooking, or grilling in the park. While I would not say that you can truly learn the art of the flame when working with a portable grill (think about a countertop electric grill), they are usually fairly inexpensive and can be super convenient.

SMOKERS

Smokers are an excellent resource for those who are masters of the flame. While charcoal and gas grills are great for beginners, the smoker will take your grilling to a new level. When you think of classic backcountry barbecue brisket, baby back ribs, and sausage, odds are they were prepared on a smoker. The smoker truly brings out that amazing barbecue flavor by cooking the meats over low temperatures with lots of smoke. These are definitely for the master griller.

OPEN FLAME

My personal preference for barbecueing is an uncovered flame. Toward the beginning of my grilling adventures, my father and I started out working on an open-flame firepit in the backyard. Our pit was a massive iron pot that we discovered buried in the ground. After a whole lot of restoration, this thing was ready to fire. We would prepare the grill by sourcing firewood, building an open fire in our backyard pit, and then adding a grill grate to the top of it. An uncovered grill lets you truly understand how different heats will cook the meat, and ultimately master the open flame.

STARTERS

STARTERS

STARTERS ARE OFTEN FORGOTTEN when it comes to family dinners and gatherings. While appetizers are traditionally served in small portions before the main course, they are in no way something that should be given little thought. Starters pave the way for the perfect grilled dinner. They not only give your guests a taste of what's to come, they also keep everyone around the table for hours, creating the perfect setting for a memorable gathering.

Grilled appetizers always seem to be the heartiest dishes, as well as the most snacked on. Showcasing the smoky atmosphere and warming aroma of the grill, these appetizers work perfectly as snacks for your guests while you work on the main dish—just don't expect many leftovers.

CLASSIC BUFFALO WINGS

Makes 4 to 6 servings / Active Time: 15 minutes / Total Time: 2 hours and 30 minutes

Perfect for a Sunday spent watching football, this dish never gets old. For this recipe, I decided to give the wings a boost by adding a couple cups of soaked wood chips to the coals. While this is optional, I strongly recommend it.

1 Place the chicken wings on a roasting pan and put it in the refrigerator. Let rest for at least 2 hours so that the skin on the wings tightens. This will promote a crisper wing.

2 One hour before grilling, place the wood chips into a bowl of water and let soak.

3 A half hour before grilling, bring your gas or charcoal grill to high heat.

4 To make the buffalo sauce, in a small saucepan, add the clarified butter and warm over medium heat. Once hot, add the garlic and cook until golden, about 2 minutes. Next, mix all of the remaining ingredients, except for the celery, into the pan and simmer for about 3 minutes. Then, remove the pan from heat and place the contents in a large bowl.

5 Remove the chicken wings from the refrigerator and toss with the buffalo sauce in the large bowl.

6 Once the grill is ready, at about 450°F with the coals lightly covered with ash, scatter the wood chips over the coals or place them in a smoker box and then place the chicken wings on the grill with a good amount of space between them. Cover the grill and cook for about 2 to 3 minutes on each side, frequently basting each wing with the remaining buffalo sauce. Remove from grill when the skin is crispy.

7 Place on a large serving platter and serve warm alongside the celery.

TOOLS

2 to 3 cups hickory or oak wood chips

Smoker box (for gas grills)

INGREDIENTS

2 pounds chicken wings, split

2 tablespoons butter, clarified

3 garlic cloves, minced

¼ teaspoon cayenne pepper

¼ teaspoon paprika

2 teaspoons Tabasco™

¼ cup Frank's Cayenne Pepper Sauce

1 head of celery, stalks cut into 3-inch pieces

CHORIZO-STUFFED MUSHROOMS

Makes 8 to 10 servings / Active Time: 25 minutes / Total Time: 50 minutes

These stuffed mushrooms can be very filling, so try not to eat too many of them. The Spanish chorizo has a strong spice to it and pairs well with a glass of red wine.

1 Bring your gas or charcoal grill to medium heat. Leave a cast-iron skillet on the grill while heating so that it develops a faint, smoky flavor.

2 While you are waiting, add the chorizo to a food processor and puree into a thick paste. Remove and set aside.

3 Once the grill is ready, at about 350°F to 400°F with the coals lightly covered with ash, brush the mushroom caps with 2 tablespoons of olive oil. Next, place the mushroom caps on the grill and cook for about 2 minutes until the tops have browned. Remove from the grill and place on a baking sheet.

4 Next, add the remaining ¼ cup of olive oil to the cast-iron skillet, followed by the onion and cherry tomatoes. Cook until the onion is translucent, about 2 minutes, and then stir in the pureed chorizo. Continue to cook until the chorizo is lightly browned, about 3 minutes. Then, add in the chicken broth and parsley. Cook for only a minute or so longer, and then remove from heat.

5 Using a spoon, fill the mushroom caps with the chorizo mixture. Move the baking sheet to a cool side of the grill and cook for about 15 minutes until the chorizo has browned. Remove from the grill, season with black pepper and sea salt, and serve hot.

TOOLS

Cast-iron skillet

Food processor

Baking sheet

INGREDIENTS

1 link of Spanish chorizo, casing removed

14 white mushrooms, stemmed

¼ cup plus 2 tablespoons olive oil

1 medium white onion, finely chopped

4 cherry tomatoes, quartered

¼ cup chicken broth

1 small bunch of parsley, finely chopped

Coarsely ground black pepper

Sea salt

SAUSAGE-STUFFED JALAPEÑOS

Makes 5 to 6 servings / Active Time: 20 minutes / Total Time: 1 hour

Grilled stuffed jalapeños are simple and quick to prepare. Although the jalapeños usually contain a bit of heat, when you remove the seeds and grill them, that heat is toned down. Pick up organic pork sausage from a local butcher, if possible. It never fails!

1 Bring your gas or charcoal grill to medium heat. Leave a cast-iron skillet on the grill while heating so that it develops a faint, smoky flavor.

2 Once the grill is ready, at 400°F with the coals lightly covered with ash, heat the olive oil in the skillet and then add the pork sausage. Cook until the sausage is no longer pink but evenly brown.

3 When the sausage is nearly cooked through, add the garlic and onion and cook until translucent, about 2 to 3 minutes. Stir in the red bell peppers and the cherry tomatoes and cook for another 2 minutes or so. Transfer the sausage mixture from the grill and let rest.

4 Arrange the halves of the jalapeño peppers evenly on a baking sheet. Using a spoon, fill the cavities of the peppers with the sausage mixture. Transfer to the grill and cook, covered, for about 20 minutes until lightly browned. Remove from the grill, season with pepper and salt, and serve immediately.

VARIATION

After filling the jalapeños with the sausage mixture, wrap each jalapeño half with a thick-cut slice of bacon. Using a toothpick, pierce each wrapped jalapeño through its middle so that the bacon doesn't unravel while grilling. Grill for about 20 minutes until the bacon is crisp and browned.

TOOLS

Cast-iron skillet

Baking sheet

INGREDIENTS

2 tablespoons olive oil

1 pound ground pork sausage

2 garlic cloves, minced

¼ small red onion, minced

3 tablespoons red bell pepper, minced

8 cherry tomatoes, minced

12 to 16 jalapeño peppers, halved and seeded

Coarsely ground black pepper

Sea salt

SMOKED SPICY CHICKEN WINGS

Makes 4 to 6 servings / Active Time: 30 minutes / Total Time: 3 hours

These chicken wings are great for warm summer evenings with friends. I recommend serving alongside celery and some Shishito Peppers (see page 385).

1 Place the chicken wings on a roasting pan and put it in the refrigerator. Let rest for at least 2 hours so that the skin on the wings tightens. This will promote a crisper wing.

2 One hour before grilling, add the wood chips to a bowl of water and let soak.

3 A half hour before grilling, bring your gas or charcoal grill to high heat.

4 While the grill heats, remove the wings from the refrigerator and place in a large bowl. Toss with the 2 tablespoons of olive oil.

5 In a medium bowl, combine all of the remaining ingredients.

6 Next, place the seasoning in the large bowl with the chicken wings and toss evenly, making sure that each wing has an equal amount of seasoning.

7 Once the grill is ready, at about 450°F with the coals lightly covered with ash, scatter the wood chips over the coals or place them in a smoker box, and then place the chicken wings on the grill with a good amount of space between them. Cover the grill and cook for about 2 to 3 minutes on each side. Remove from grill when the skin is crispy. Serve immediately.

TOOLS

2 to 3 cups hickory or oak wood chips

Smoker box (for gas grills)

INGREDIENTS

2 pounds chicken wings, split

2 tablespoons olive oil

Juice from ½ small lime

3 garlic cloves, finely chopped

2 tablespoons flat-leaf parsley, finely chopped

1 tablespoon ground cumin

2 teaspoons paprika

1 teaspoon ground cinnamon

1 teaspoon turmeric

1 teaspoon red pepper flakes

½ teaspoon onion powder

Coarsely ground black pepper

Sea salt

CLASSIC ANTIPASTO

Makes 4 servings / Active Time: 15 minutes / Total Time: 1 hour

This dish is best served at large gatherings. This is just a base recipe; feel free to add more options if you want.

1 Stem the cherry tomatoes and place in a small bowl. Submerge in ½ cup olive oil and let marinate for 30 minutes to 1 hour.

2 In a small bowl, combine the assorted olives, garlic, thyme, and 2 tablespoons of olive oil and let marinate for 30 minutes to 1 hour.

3 Take a small frying pan and place it over medium-high heat. Add the remaining 2 tablespoons of olive oil. When hot, stir in the walnuts and almonds and toast for about 2 minutes. Remove and set aside.

4 Arrange the prosciutto and hard salami on a large platter and season lightly with coarsely cracked black pepper.

5 Arrange the walnuts, almonds, tomatoes, olives, and, if desired, assorted cheeses on the platter. Serve immediately.

INGREDIENTS

12 cherry tomatoes

½ cup plus 4 tablespoons olive oil

½ cup assorted olives

½ teaspoon garlic, chopped

Leaves from 1 sprig of thyme

¼ cup walnuts

¼ cup almonds

½ pound fresh prosciutto, shaved

8 to 10 thick slices of hard salami

Coarsely ground black pepper

Assorted cheeses (optional)

SHRIMP COCKTAIL

Makes 10 to 12 servings / Active Time: 10 minutes / Total Time: 1 hour and 30 minutes

In this classic summer dish, we build upon a standard tomato sauce to arrive at a fresh cocktail sauce. This sauce is best enjoyed chilled, perhaps with a glass of white wine.

INGREDIENTS

2 pounds precooked shrimp, deveined and shelled

2 cups organic tomato sauce

1 to 2 tablespoons fresh horseradish, depending on taste

1 teaspoon Dijon mustard

Juice from ¼ small lemon

Coarsely ground black pepper

Sea salt

1 large lemon, quartered

1 Arrange the shrimp on a large platter and place in the refrigerator. Chill for at least 1 hour before serving.

2 In a medium bowl, combine all of the remaining ingredients except for the quartered lemon. Place in the refrigerator and chill for about 30 minutes.

3 Place the bowl of cocktail sauce, along with the wedges of lemon, in the center of the shrimp platter. Serve chilled.

DEVILED EGGS

Makes 6 servings / Active Time: 15 minutes / Total Time: 30 minutes

This recipe is very straightforward and is easy to adapt for big groups. The real kick comes from the Dijon mustard, which pairs well with the bacon and sets high standards for your main course. Keep in mind that this is a basic recipe, so you can add any other seasonings that come to mind.

1   In a small food processor, add the 2 egg yolks and the lemon juice and puree for 30 seconds. Gradually add the light olive oil until you reach a thick, mayonnaise-like consistency. It is extremely important to add the light olive oil slowly to the processor. If you go too quickly, you will not reach the desired consistency.

2   Fill a medium saucepan with water. Carefully add the 10 eggs to the saucepan and place over medium heat. When the water reaches a boil, pull the eggs from the hot water and rinse under cool water. Let rest for a few minutes, and then peel back the shells.

3   Slice the eggs in half lengthwise. Using a fork, transfer the egg yolks from the eggs and place in a small bowl. Whisk in the mayonnaise-like mixture, Dijon mustard, and parsley, and then season with pepper and sea salt. Set aside.

4   Place a medium frying pan over medium-high heat. Add the slices of bacon to the pan and cook until crispy, a few minutes on each side. If you would like to add a smoky flavor to the bacon, consider smoking the bacon on the grill. Transfer the bacon to a cutting board and chop into bits. Whisk into the mixture.

5   Spoon the mixture from the small bowl back into the egg whites. If desired, garnish with paprika and chopped chives. Serve chilled.

TOOLS

Food processor

Saucepan

Frying pan

INGREDIENTS

2 egg yolks, at room temperature

Juice from ¼ lemon

1 cup light olive oil

10 large eggs

2 tablespoons Dijon mustard

2 tablespoons fresh parsley, finely chopped

Coarsely ground black pepper

Sea salt

6 thick-cut slices of bacon

1 teaspoon paprika (optional)

3 chives, finely chopped (optional)

BEEFSTEAK TOMATOES WITH BASIL AND BALSAMIC VINAIGRETTE

Makes 4 to 6 servings / Active Time: 10 minutes / Total Time: 10 minutes

I recommend serving this before a heavy main dish, as it is not too filling and offers a tasty hint of what's to come.

INGREDIENTS

4 beefsteak tomatoes, sliced into ½-inch rounds

½ cup fresh basil leaves

1 tablespoon olive oil

1 tablespoon balsamic vinegar

Coarsely ground black pepper

Sea salt

1 Place the sliced beefsteak tomatoes on a platter, then layer with the basil leaves.

2 In a small glass, combine the olive oil and balsamic vinegar, and then spread it evenly across the tomatoes and basil.

3 Season with black pepper and sea salt, and then serve immediately.

SARDINES WITH LEMON AND HERBS

Makes 6 servings / Active Time: 15 minutes / Total Time: 40 minutes

Sardines have a strong "fishiness" to them. As such, be sure to serve these with a crisp white wine to help the taste buds mellow out before the main course.

1 Line the bottom of a small baking dish with the sardines. Submerge the sardines in the fresh lemon juice and olive oil, and then transfer to the refrigerator. Let marinate for 30 minutes.

2 A half hour before grilling, bring your gas or charcoal grill to medium heat.

3 While waiting, combine the garlic, shallot, parsley, and cilantro in a small bowl. Set next to the grill.

4 Once the grill is ready, at about 400°F with the coals lightly covered with ash, remove the sardines from the refrigerator and place over direct heat. Season the tops of the sardines with the herb mixture, and then grill for 1 to 2 minutes. Flip and season once more, cooking for 1 to 2 more minutes. Remove when the centers are opaque.

5 Transfer the sardines to a large cutting board and let rest for 5 minutes. Season with pepper and salt and serve warm.

INGREDIENTS

Fresh sardines, scaled, gutted, and cleaned

Juice from 2 large lemons

¼ cup olive oil

3 garlic cloves, finely chopped

1 small shallot, finely chopped

2 tablespoons flat-leaf parsley, finely chopped

1 tablespoon cilantro, finely chopped

Coarsely ground black pepper

Sea salt

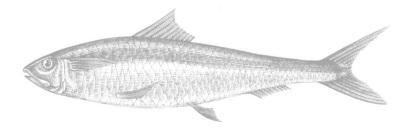

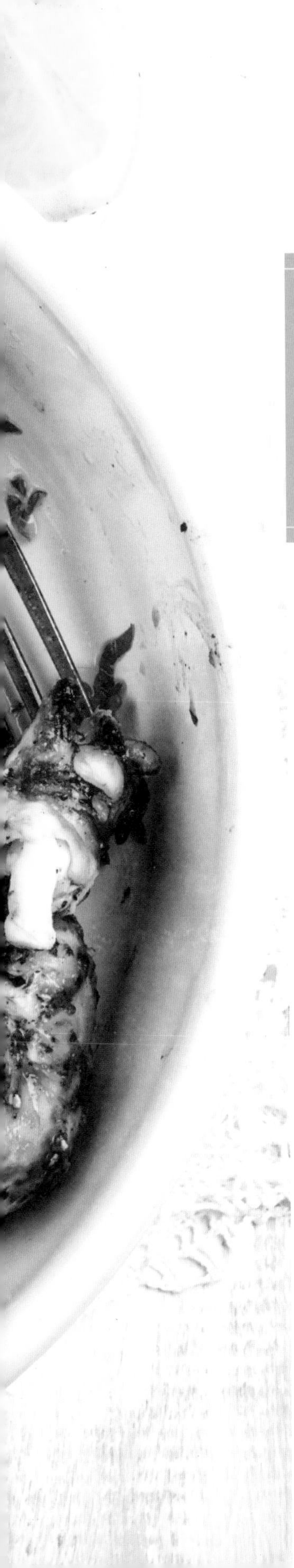

CALAMARI

Makes 6 servings / **Active Time: 15 minutes** / **Total Time: 2 hours**

Great as an appetizer or snack, grilled calamari is best when served family style. Serve in a large dish with Marinara Sauce (see pages 236–37) on the side and allow everyone to take what they like.

TOOLS

Cast-iron skillet

INGREDIENTS

Juice from 1 lemon

¼ cup olive oil

2 garlic cloves, finely chopped

Leaves from 2 sprigs of oregano

Coarsely ground black pepper

Sea salt

2 pounds fresh squid, tentacles separated from bodies

1   Combine the lemon juice, olive oil, garlic, and oregano in a large bowl. Season with coarsely ground black pepper and sea salt. Add the squid to the bowl and let marinate for 1 to 2 hours.

2   Bring your gas or charcoal grill to medium heat. Leave a cast-iron skillet on the grill while heating so that it develops a faint, smoky flavor.

3   Once the grill is ready, at about 400°F with the coals lightly covered with ash, place the squid tentacles and rings in the skillet and cook until opaque, about 3 to 4 minutes. When finished, transfer the squid to a large cutting board and let stand at room temperature for 5 minutes before serving.

EDAMAME

Makes 4 servings / Active Time: 10 minutes / Total Time: 15 minutes

Edamame beans are actually whole, immature soybeans. High in protein, fiber, antioxidants, and vitamin K, they are also extremely healthy. But don't be scared off by all of those health benefits—with a touch of smoke from the grill and a bit of salt and pepper, these are perfect for munching on before dinner.

TOOLS

Cast-iron skillet

INGREDIENTS

1 pound edamame pods

2 teaspoons extra virgin olive oil

Coarsely ground black pepper

Sea salt

1 Place a medium cast-iron skillet on your gas or charcoal grill and bring the grill to medium heat. Leave the grill covered while heating, as this will add a faint smoky flavor to the skillet.

2 Toss the edamame pods in olive oil, then season lightly with black pepper and sea salt.

3 Once the grill is ready, about 400°F, transfer the edamame pods into the cast-iron skillet. Let the edamame cook for about 30 seconds, untouched, and then stir frequently for about 4 minutes until blistered and browned.

4 Transfer the edamame from the skillet to a serving bowl and enjoy immediately.

MIXED VEGETABLE BRUSCHETTA

Makes 6 servings / Active Time: 10 minutes / Total Time: 25 minutes

Bruschetta is a wonderful appetizer that can be adjusted in any way you like and is a great way to showcase fresh vegetables. I love making this in the summertime when the zucchini is garden-fresh and plentiful.

1 Bring your gas or charcoal grill to medium heat.

2 In a large bowl, add the zucchini, summer squash, celery, peppers, onion, and tomato. Add ¼ cup of the olive oil and the minced garlic and toss to coat evenly.

3 Once the grill is ready, at about 400°F with the coals lightly covered with ash, place the tomato and the vegetables directly on the grill. Grill for about 8 to 10 minutes, turning the vegetables occasionally. Once the vegetables are tender, remove from heat and let cool on a cutting board.

4 Chop the vegetables into bite-sized pieces, mix together, and set aside in a large bowl.

5 Brush the bread slices on both sides with olive oil. Grill each piece for about 1 minute per side until the bread is lightly toasted.

6 Spoon the grilled veggies onto the toast and sprinkle basil leaves, oregano, and parsley over the top. Serve and enjoy.

VARIATION

If you want to beef this dish up a bit, sprinkle bits of cooked bacon over the bruschetta. To cook the bacon, add a cast-iron skillet to the grill while it is heating, that way the cast-iron skillet heats up as well. Once hot, add the bacon to the skillet and cook for about 2 to 3 minutes per side until browned.

INGREDIENTS

1 small zucchini, cut into ¾-inch slices

1 small summer squash, cut into ¾-inch slices

1 celery stalk, cut into ¾-inch slices

2 bell peppers, cut into wedges

1 medium red onion, cut into wedges

1 medium tomato, cut into wedges

½ cup olive oil

5 garlic cloves, minced

15 (¼-inch thick) slices of French bread

6 fresh basil leaves, torn

1 teaspoon oregano, minced

1 teaspoon parsley, minced

ZUCCHINI NACHOS

Makes 4 servings / Active Time: 10 minutes / Total Time: 25 minutes

This is a fun twist on a classic starter, as the lightness of the zucchini is a great base for the traditional nacho toppings. This is sure to please everyone at the table.

1 Prepare your nachos by slicing the zucchini into ¼-inch-thick slices, just like chips.

2 Place sliced zucchini in a medium bowl and toss with olive oil.

3 Preheat grill to medium heat. Once the grill is ready, at about 400°F with the coals lightly covered with ash, place the zucchini chips on the grill. Cook the chips until the zucchini is tender, about 4 to 5 minutes. Sprinkle cheese over the zucchini chips and continue cooking until the cheese is slightly melted, about 1 minute.

4 Place cooked chips on a large platter and top with black beans, tomato, avocado, onions, cilantro, and lime juice. Season with coarsely ground black pepper and sea salt and serve.

VARIATION

Add chopped chicken to the nachos for a protein boost. Simply season and grill 1 chicken breast alongside the zucchini nachos, cooking the chicken breast for about 4 to 5 minutes per side. When the chicken is tender and juicy, remove, slice, and sprinkle on top of the nachos.

INGREDIENTS

2 medium zucchini

¼ cup olive oil

1 cup cheddar cheese, shredded

1 (15 oz.) can of black beans, drained

1 large tomato, chopped

1 large avocado, sliced

2 green onions, finely chopped

¼ cup cilantro, finely chopped

Juice from 1 lime wedge

Coarsely ground black pepper

Sea salt

NUTTY STUFFED MUSHROOMS

Makes 4 servings / Active Time: 15 minutes / Total Time: 35 minutes

These stuffed mushrooms make a great meal or snack, depending on how many you want to eat. I like to make them using fresh mushrooms and basil leaves for that added savory note.

1 Preheat your gas or charcoal grill to medium heat.

2 Prepare 2 large sheets of aluminum foil. Make sure foil is large enough for all 24 mushrooms to rest on. The second piece of foil will be used to cover the top and to create a packet.

3 Combine the green onions, basil, and nuts, and then stuff the mushrooms with the mixture. Drizzle the mushrooms with olive oil and sprinkle with the cheeses, pepper, and salt. Set each stuffed mushroom neatly on the bottom sheet of aluminum foil. When all 24 stuffed mushrooms are placed evenly on the foil, cover with the second sheet of foil. Curl the edges so that the mushrooms are "sealed" in the foil.

4 Once the grill is ready, at about 400°F with the coals lightly covered with ash, place the mushroom packet on the grill and cook for 20 minutes until mushrooms become tender.

5 After 20 minutes, remove the mushroom packet from the grill. Open the packet, check to make sure the mushrooms are tender, and serve.

VARIATION

Consider adding a little meat to the mushrooms. Take 6 to 8 slices of deli salami and chop them into small pieces. Add the chopped salami to the green onion, basil, and nut mixture, and then stuff into the mushrooms.

TOOLS

Aluminum foil

INGREDIENTS

24 cremini mushrooms, stemmed

4 green onions, chopped

Fresh basil leaves, diced

2 tablespoons pine nuts, walnuts, or hazelnuts, diced

¼ cup olive oil

¼ cup Parmesan cheese, grated

¼ cup mozzarella, shredded

Coarsely ground black pepper

Sea salt

SOUPS & SALADS

SOUPS & SALADS

SOUPS AND GRILLING are rarely paired together, but when they are they produce some of the most memorable meals. Preparing soups on the grill will take time and considerable attention. If you are using a charcoal grill, that means restocking the coals about every hour. When making soups on the grill, it is extremely important to find a quality charcoal that will give you the perfect mix between smoke and heat. In addition, be sure to have several cups of soaked hickory or oak wood chips alongside the grill to toss onto the coals when needed.

There's one secret to cooking soups and stews on the grill: a cast-iron Dutch oven. The Dutch oven allows for a slow braising of the ingredients, as the cast-iron maintains a consistent heat and allows for even cooking. In fact, the more you use your cast-iron Dutch oven, the more flavor it will develop. A high-quality Dutch oven is well worth the investment, especially if you cook earthy dishes made with the freshest ingredients possible, as it takes on the best of every meal.

Both the soups and salads in this chapter take advantage of the best parts of grilling outdoors. You can't replicate the Portuguese Kale and Sausage Soup (see page 48) or our Chicken Tomatillo Soup (see page 59) on a stove. We wanted to add real smoky notes to our Smoked Tomato Basil Soup (see page 56) and Smoked Manhattan Clam Chowder (see pages 54–55), so our recipes require that you stoke the coals with hickory or oak wood chips. To make sure you get the smoky flavor you're after, cover the grill while cooking, aligning the air vent away from the Dutch oven so that the smoke billows around the soup.

The salads feature grilled ingredients and toppings that bring the iconic taste of the grill to your table, such as sunflower seeds toasted in a cast-iron skillet and paired with charred beets. Maple wood chips add a unique element to bacon, which would be perfect in our Frisée Salad with Bacon and Eggs (see page 67) and our Sweet Potato Soup with Bacon and Walnuts (see page 51).

CHICKEN STOCK

Makes about 12 cups / Active Time: 11 hours / Total Time: 12 hours

Made with all parts of the chicken, a slow-cooked stock is rich in minerals essential to good health, including calcium, magnesium, phosphorus, silicon, and sulfur. A great stock lays the foundation for an even greater meal.

1   If you are using a whole chicken, cut off the neck, wings, and legs and cut them into pieces. Cut the rest of the chicken pieces into chunks.

2   Place a large Dutch oven on your gas or charcoal grill and bring to medium heat. Leave the grill covered while heating, as it will add a faint smoky flavor to the Dutch oven.

3   Once the grill is ready, at about 400°F with the coals lightly covered with ash, place all of the chicken components in the Dutch oven and top with all of the vegetables. Cover with water and vinegar. Cover the Dutch oven, and let the meat and vegetables cook in the liquid for 30 minutes to 1 hour.

4   Tending the coals every 30 minutes, cook for 2 to 3 hours. Remove the cover and skim off any fat that has risen to the top.

5   Replace the cover and reduce the grill to low heat. Continue to add coals to the fire and cook for about 8 to 10 hours. Add the parsley in the last 15 minutes or so.

6   When cooking is complete, remove the solids with a slotted spoon and discard. Any drippings in the bowl can go back into the stock. Transfer the stock to a large bowl and refrigerate. Once the fat has congealed on top, skim it off and transfer the stock to several smaller containers with tight-fitting lids.

VARIATION

For an even richer stock, broil the chicken pieces for about 3 minutes per side before adding them to the soup.

TOOLS

Dutch oven

INGREDIENTS

1 whole free-range chicken, or 2 to 3 pounds of carcass (necks, backs, breastbones, legs, wings)

Chicken gizzards

2 to 4 chicken feet (optional)

1 large onion, chopped

2 carrots, peeled and sliced

2 celery stalks, chopped

4 quarts cold water

2 tablespoons vinegar

1 bunch of parsley, chopped

PORTUGUESE KALE AND SAUSAGE SOUP

Makes 6 servings / Active Time: 45 minutes / Total Time: 1 hour

If you go to your local farmers market or butcher, you should be able to find an organic sausage that will truly bring this soup to life.

1 Place a large Dutch oven on your gas or charcoal grill and bring to medium heat. Leave the grill covered while heating, as it will add a faint smoky flavor to the pot.

2 Once the grill is ready, at about 400°F with the coals lightly covered with ash, add the olive oil, followed by the onion, garlic, and sausage pieces. Cook until the onion and sausage have browned, about 7 minutes. Remove the sausage from the Dutch oven and set aside.

3 Next, stir the pepper flakes, stock, and water into the pot and bring to a boil. Cook, uncovered, for about 20 minutes. Add the kale and boil for about 5 more minutes until tender. Stir in the sausage and cook for about 2 more minutes.

4 Remove the Dutch oven from the grill and season with black pepper and sea salt. Serve hot.

TOOLS

Dutch oven

INGREDIENTS

2 tablespoons olive oil

1 medium yellow onion, finely chopped

1 garlic clove, finely chopped

¾ pound pork or chicken sausage, cut into ½-inch pieces

¼ teaspoon red pepper flakes

3 cups Chicken Stock (see page 47)

2 cups water

1 pound fresh kale, stemmed and chopped

Coarsely ground black pepper

Sea salt

SWEET POTATO SOUP WITH BACON AND WALNUTS

Makes 6 servings / Active Time: 45 minutes / Total Time: 1 hour and 30 minutes

For an extra touch, smoke the bacon and walnuts with maple wood chips. This soup takes a relatively short amount of time to prepare and is perfect for a last-minute meal. I recommend serving with a Pinot Grigio or Sauvignon Blanc.

1. One hour before grilling, soak the maple wood chips in water.

2. Next, place a large Dutch oven on your gas or charcoal grill and bring to medium heat. Leave the grill covered while heating, as it will add a faint smoky flavor to the pot.

3. Once the grill is ready, at about 400°F with the coals lightly covered with ash, throw the wood chips over the coals or in a smoker box and cover the grill. Once the grill is smoking, add the bacon to the Dutch oven, close the lid, and cook until crispy, about 4 minutes. Meanwhile, place a sheet of aluminum foil on the grill and place the walnuts on it; toast for a couple of minutes, remove, and set aside. Transfer the bacon to a plate covered with paper towels and then chop into ½-inch pieces. Set aside.

4. Add the olive oil to the Dutch oven, followed by the shallot and cook for about 5 minutes until translucent. Add the garlic and cook for another minute until golden.

5. Once the garlic is golden, add the sweet potatoes, Chicken Stock, and water to the pot and cook for about 15 minutes until the sweet potatoes are easily pierced with a fork.

6. Stir in the cinnamon and nutmeg and then remove the Dutch oven from the heat.

7. Remove the bacon from the pot with a slotted spoon. Using a large food processor or immersion blender, blend the soup into a desired consistency, and then season with black pepper and sea salt. Finally, top with the bacon and toasted walnuts and serve warm.

TOOLS

2 cups maple wood chips

Dutch oven

Smoker box (for gas grill)

Aluminum foil

INGREDIENTS

8 thick-cut slices of bacon, trimmed of excess fat

1 cup walnuts

1 teaspoon olive oil

1 medium shallot, finely chopped

4 garlic cloves, finely chopped

2 to 3 large sweet potatoes, peeled and sliced into thin ½-inch strips

3 cups Chicken Stock (see page 47)

1 cup water

⅛ teaspoon ground cinnamon

⅛ teaspoon ground nutmeg

Coarsely ground black pepper

Sea salt

SPLIT PEA SOUP WITH HAM

Makes 6 servings / Active Time: 1 hour and 30 minutes / Total Time: 2 hours and 30 minutes

Here is one of my favorite recipes from my mother, though she will always make it best. This filling recipe is perfect for just when the weather turns cold, a fitting send-off for grilling season.

1 Place a large Dutch oven on your gas or charcoal grill and bring to medium heat. Leave the grill covered while heating, as it will add a faint smoky flavor to the pot.

2 Once the grill is ready, at about 400°F with the coals lightly covered with ash, add the olive oil to the Dutch oven, followed by the carrots and onion. Cook for about 5 to 7 minutes until the carrots are tender and the onion is translucent. Stir in the garlic and cook for another minute.

3 Add the split peas, red pepper flakes, and ham to the Dutch oven, and then cover with the 6 cups of water (you may need more or less depending on the size of the Dutch oven and ham). Cover and cook until the peas have fully cooked, about 1½ to 2 hours. Be sure to restock the coals while cooking.

4 Add the thyme leaves and cook for a few more minutes before removing from grill. Let the soup rest for about 15 minutes so that it can thicken, and then season with black pepper and sea salt. Serve hot.

TOOLS

Dutch oven

INGREDIENTS

1 tablespoon olive oil

1 cup carrots, chopped into ¼-inch pieces

1 medium yellow onion, finely chopped

3 garlic cloves, minced

1 pound dried split peas

¼ teaspoon red pepper flakes

1 (4 pound) ready-to-eat ham

6 cups water

Leaves from 2 sprigs of thyme

Coarsely ground black pepper

Sea salt

TOOLS

2 cups hickory or oak wood chips

Dutch oven

Smoker box (for gas grill)

INGREDIENTS

4 thick-cut slices of bacon

1 tablespoon olive oil

1 medium yellow onion, finely chopped

3 celery stalks, diced into ¼-inch segments

1 green pepper, stemmed, seeded, and diced

2 garlic cloves, minced

2 cups fresh clam juice

6 (6.5 oz.) cans of whole clams

2 cups canned diced tomatoes, with juice

Leaves from 2 sprigs of thyme

1 tablespoon flat-leaf parsley

Coarsely ground black pepper

Sea salt

SMOKED MANHATTAN CLAM CHOWDER

Makes 6 servings / Active Time: 35 minutes / Total Time: 1 hour and 20 minutes

The cream-based version is more popular, but the earthy flavors in this tomato-based take are perfect for the grill.

1 One hour before grilling, soak the wood chips in water.

2 Next, place a large Dutch oven on your gas or charcoal grill and bring to medium heat. Leave the grill covered while heating, as this will add a faint smoky flavor to the Dutch oven.

3 Once the grill is ready, at about 400°F with the coals lightly covered with ash, throw the wood chips over the coals or in a smoker box and cover the grill. Once the grill is smoking, add the bacon to the Dutch oven, close the lid, and cook until crispy, about 4 minutes. Transfer the bacon to a plate covered with paper towels and let cool. When cool enough to handle, chop into bite-sized pieces.

4 Add the olive oil to the Dutch oven and cook until warm. Next, add the yellow onion, celery, and green pepper and cook until the onion is translucent and the pepper is tender, about 7 minutes. Stir in the garlic and sear until golden, about a minute.

5 Next, stir in the clam juice, bacon, clams, and canned tomatoes and cook until the tomatoes have broken down slightly, about 10 to 15 minutes.

6 Stir in the thyme and parsley. Remove the Dutch oven from the heat and let rest for 5 minutes. Season with black pepper and sea salt and serve hot.

VARIATION

You may prefer to use 3 medium fresh plum tomatoes instead of canned tomatoes. If you do, be sure to add 1 cup of water to the recipe.

SMOKED TOMATO BASIL SOUP

Makes 6 servings / Active Time: 2 hours / Total Time: 3 hours

Since the smoke can add an overpowering aroma to the soup, I encourage you to add the wood chips to the coals for only about 15 minutes before the soup is finished.

1 Place a large Dutch oven on your gas or charcoal grill and bring to medium heat. Leave the grill covered while heating, as it will add a faint smoky flavor to the Dutch oven.

2 While waiting, place the wood chips in a bowl of water and let soak for at least 1 hour.

3 Once the grill is ready, at about 400°F with the coals lightly covered with ash, add the 3 tablespoons of olive oil to the Dutch oven, followed by the yellow onions, and then cook for about 5 to 7 minutes. When the onions are lightly brown, stir in the garlic and cook until golden, being careful not to brown, about 2 minutes.

4 Next, add the halved tomatoes and the remaining ¼ cup of olive oil. Bring to a simmer and cook for about 5 minutes. Mash the tomatoes with a fork, and then stir in the Chicken Stock, clarified butter, basil leaves, and thyme and simmer for about 25 minutes.

5 After about 25 minutes, throw the soaked wood chips onto the coals or in a smoker box and cover the grill, letting the soup cook for 15 more minutes.

6 Remove the Dutch oven from the grill and let rest for a few minutes. If you would like a thinner texture, puree the soup in a food processor until you reach the desired consistency. Season with black pepper and sea salt and serve warm.

TOOLS

Dutch oven

2 cups hickory or oak wood chips

Smoker box (for gas grill)

INGREDIENTS

¼ cup plus 3 tablespoons olive oil

2 large yellow onions, finely chopped

5 garlic cloves, finely chopped

2 to 3 pounds plum tomatoes, seeded and halved

4 cups Chicken Stock (see page 47)

3 tablespoons butter, clarified

4 cups fresh basil leaves

Leaves from 2 sprigs of thyme

Coarsely ground black pepper

Sea salt

CHICKEN TOMATILLO SOUP

Makes 6 servings / Active Time: 30 minutes / Total Time: 45 minutes

With tangy tomatillos and spicy jalapeño, this soup has enough flavor to serve as a main course.

1 Place a large Dutch oven on your gas or charcoal grill and bring to medium heat. Leave the grill covered while heating, as it will add a faint smoky flavor to the Dutch oven.

2 While waiting for the grill, puree the tomatillos and jalapeño in a food processor with lime juice and set aside.

3 Once the grill is ready, at about 400°F with the coals lightly covered with ash, heat the olive oil in the Dutch oven. Once hot, add the chicken breasts and cook until browned, about 2 to 3 minutes per side. Remove and set aside.

4 Add the white onion and scallions to the Dutch oven and cook until the onion is translucent, about 5 minutes. Stir in the garlic and cook until golden, about 1 minute.

5 Next, add the Chicken Stock to the Dutch oven, followed by the mixture of tomatillos and jalapeño. Bring to a boil and then reduce heat and simmer for about 15 minutes.

6 On a cutting board, dice the chicken and add to the soup along with the cilantro. Boil until the chicken is cooked through, about 5 more minutes, and then remove the Dutch oven from the grill. Season with black pepper and sea salt and serve with sour cream, if desired.

VARIATION

If you would like a bit more spice, substitute the jalapeño for a habanero pepper.

TOOLS

Food processor

Dutch oven

INGREDIENTS

3 tomatillos, husks removed and rinsed

1 jalapeño pepper, stemmed and seeded to taste

Juice from ½ small lime

1 tablespoon olive oil

2 skinless, boneless chicken breasts

1 medium white onion, chopped

3 scallions, finely chopped

2 garlic cloves, minced

4 cups Chicken Stock (see page 47)

¼ cup fresh cilantro, minced

Coarsely ground black pepper

Sea salt

Sour cream, for serving (optional)

CLASSIC CAESAR SALAD

Makes 6 servings / Active Time: 10 minutes / Total Time: 25 minutes

Anchovy fillets are an essential ingredient in the Classic Caesar Salad, as their fishy aroma complements the lightness of the olive oil.

1 Rinse the heads of romaine lettuce and dry thoroughly. Chop roughly, place in refrigerator, and set aside.

2 In a small bowl, whisk the minced garlic, lemon juice, and egg until blended. Whisk in the anchovy fillets and Dijon mustard until the anchovies have been completely incorporated into the dressing.

3 Gradually whisk in the olive oil and then season with black pepper and salt. Place the dressing in the refrigerator for about 15 minutes and then pour over the chilled lettuce. Top with the grated Parmesan and croutons before serving.

VARIATION

Top this salad with grilled chicken or smoked bacon for a light dinner.

INGREDIENTS

3 heads of romaine lettuce

2 garlic cloves, minced

Juice from ½ small lemon

1 large egg

4 anchovy fillets

1 teaspoon Dijon mustard

½ cup olive oil

Coarsely ground black pepper

Sea salt

Parmesan cheese, grated

Croutons

ARUGULA SALAD WITH TARRAGON-SHALLOT VINAIGRETTE

Makes 6 servings / Active Time: 10 minutes / Total Time: 15 minutes

This simple salad is quick to make and full of lovely aromatic notes from the vinaigrette.

INGREDIENTS

1 pound arugula, stemmed

1 shallot, minced

5 sprigs of tarragon, minced

Juice from ¼ small lemon

1 teaspoon Dijon mustard

½ cup olive oil

3 tablespoons red wine vinegar

Coarsely ground black pepper

Sea salt

1 Rinse the arugula and then dry thoroughly. Place in the refrigerator to chill while preparing the vinaigrette.

2 In a small bowl, whisk together the shallot, tarragon, lemon juice, and Dijon mustard, and then slowly add the olive oil and red wine vinegar.

3 Season with black pepper and sea salt and pour over the arugula. Serve immediately.

SPINACH SALAD WITH RED ONION AND MAPLE-SMOKED BACON

Makes 6 servings / Active Time: 35 minutes / Total Time: 45 minutes

This salad is perfect for summer evenings and works well when served with a seafood or poultry dish and some white wine. The layer added by the smoked bacon helps bring the entire ensemble together.

1 One hour before grilling, soak the wood chips in water.

2 Next, place a large cast-iron skillet on your gas or charcoal grill and bring to medium heat. Leave the grill covered while heating, as it will add a faint smoky flavor to the skillet.

3 While waiting, rinse the spinach and dry thoroughly. Place the spinach in a medium bowl and mix in the red onion and dried cranberries. Transfer to the refrigerator and set aside.

4 Once the grill is ready, at about 400°F with the coals lightly covered with ash, throw the wood chips over the coals or in a smoker box and cover the grill. Once the grill is smoking, add the bacon to the cast-iron skillet, close the grill's lid, and cook until crispy, about 4 minutes. Transfer the bacon to a plate covered with paper towels and then chop into ½-inch pieces. Set aside.

5 In a small bowl, whisk together the balsamic vinegar, Dijon mustard, and red pepper flakes (if using), and then gradually incorporate the olive oil. Season with black pepper and sea salt, and then mix with the spinach salad and bacon bits. If desired, top with sesame and sunflower seeds before serving.

VARIATION

Those who like the heat might want to toss in a couple pepperoncini peppers.

TOOLS

1 cup maple wood chips

Cast-iron skillet

Smoker box (for gas grill)

INGREDIENTS

1 pound spinach

1 medium red onion, sliced into ¼-inch rings

¼ cup dried cranberries

8 thick-cut slices of bacon, trimmed of excess fat

2 tablespoons balsamic vinegar

1 teaspoon Dijon mustard

1 teaspoon red pepper flakes (optional)

½ cup olive oil

Coarsely ground black pepper

Sea salt

Sesame seeds (optional)

Sunflower seeds (optional)

FRISÉE SALAD WITH BACON & EGGS

Makes 6 servings / Active Time: 15 minutes / Total Time: 40 minutes

This salad is filling enough to become the main course. I like to pair it with a side of Beets with Walnuts (see page 414) to balance the strong tanginess of the vinaigrette.

1 One hour before grilling, soak the wood chips in water.

2 Next, place a large cast-iron skillet on your gas or charcoal grill and bring to medium heat. Leave the grill covered while heating, as it will add a faint smoky flavor to the skillet.

3 Rinse the frisée and dry thoroughly. Place the frisée in a medium bowl and store it in the refrigerator.

4 Once the grill is ready, at about 400°F with the coals lightly covered with ash, throw the wood chips over the coals or in a smoker box and cover the grill. Once the grill is smoking, add the bacon to the cast-iron skillet, close the grill's lid, and cook until crispy, about 4 minutes. Transfer to a plate covered with paper towels and chop into bite-sized pieces when cool enough to handle.

5 In a small bowl, whisk together the white wine vinegar, red wine vinegar, Dijon mustard, and olive oil and then set aside.

6 If using hard-boiled eggs, peel them, slice them in half, and add to the salad. Drizzle the vinaigrette onto the frisée and then top with the bacon bits and croutons. Season with the black pepper and sea salt and serve.

TOOLS

1 cup oak or maple wood chips

Cast-iron skillet

Saucepan

Smoker box (for gas grill)

INGREDIENTS

1 pound frisée

8 thick slices of bacon, trimmed of excess fat

2 tablespoons white wine vinegar

2 tablespoons red wine vinegar

1 teaspoon Dijon mustard

2 tablespoons olive oil

3 large eggs, poached or hard-boiled

Croutons

Coarsely ground black pepper

Sea salt

BEETS AND TOASTED SUNFLOWER SEEDS OVER ARUGULA

Makes 6 servings / Active Time: 15 minutes / Total Time: 20 minutes

Beets are the perfect ingredient to add to a summer salad. Their juiciness and vibrant color, combined with the soft green of the arugula, transform the dish from a simple salad into an artistic masterpiece.

1 Rinse the arugula and then dry thoroughly. Set it aside in the refrigerator.

2 Cut the beets into quarters and then combine with ¼ cup of the olive oil in a small bowl. Let rest for 30 minutes.

3 Place a medium cast-iron skillet on your gas or charcoal grill and bring it to medium-high heat. Leave the grill covered while heating, as it will add a faint, smoky flavor to the skillet.

4 Once the grill is ready, at about 425°F, transfer the beets onto the grill (do not place them in the skillet). Grill the beets for about 10 minutes, until tender and marked. Transfer the beets to a large bowl and cover with aluminum foil.

5 Add the sunflower seeds to the cast-iron skillet and cook until browned, about 2 minutes. Remove and mix in with the beets. Set aside.

6 In a small bowl, add the remaining 2 tablespoons of olive oil and balsamic vinegar and mix thoroughly. Drizzle on top of beets and sunflower seeds, and then place over chilled arugula. Season with black pepper and sea salt before serving.

TOOLS

Cast-iron skillet

INGREDIENTS

⅓ pound arugula, rinsed and stemmed

6 medium red beets, peeled

¼ cup plus 2 tablespoons olive oil

¼ cup sunflower seeds

2 tablespoons balsamic vinegar

Coarsely ground black pepper

Sea salt

VARIATION

Add ½ cup of walnuts when you're toasting the sunflower seeds for a hint of umami.

GREEN BEAN AND ARUGULA SALAD

Makes 4 servings / Active Time: 10 minutes / Total Time: 25 minutes

This recipe gets its unique flavor from the grilled green beans and the bitterness of the arugula. Whip this up in a flash and bask in the glory of fresh vegetables.

INGREDIENTS

1 bunch of fresh green beans

1 tablespoon extra virgin olive oil

1 bunch of arugula

2 tablespoons balsamic vinegar

1 red bell pepper, minced

Coarsely ground black pepper

Sea salt

1 On a cutting board, trim the green beans, then mix with olive oil in a small bowl.

2 Preheat your grill to medium heat. Once the grill is ready, about 400°F with the coals lightly covered in ash, spread the beans over the grate. Cover the grill and cook for about 15 to 20 minutes, turning every now and then, until the beans are lightly browned.

3 Once the beans are crispy and cooked through, remove and toss with the arugula, vinegar, and bell pepper. Season with black pepper and sea salt and serve.

YELLOW SUMMER SQUASH SALAD

Makes 4 servings / Active Time: 15 minutes / Total Time: 25 minutes

Squash is perfect for those looking to amp up their salad game. Fresh vegetables and a deliciously tangy dressing make this salad a mouthwatering delight.

1 Preheat your grill to medium-high heat. In a small bowl, add the Dijon mustard, ¼ cup olive oil, balsamic vinegar, and red wine vinegar. Mix together until it has blended evenly and set aside.

2 In a small bowl, toss the squash and zucchini with the remaining olive oil and set beside your grill.

3 Once the grill is ready, at about 425°F with the coals lightly covered in ash, grill your squash and zucchini for about 6 to 8 minutes, turning every now and then. Remove from heat once grill marks are present and the vegetables are tender.

4 On a cutting board, cut the vegetables into small cubes, brush with some of the dressing, and set aside.

5 In a large serving bowl, mix together the squash and zucchini with baby spinach, cherry tomatoes, basil leaves, and mint leaves. Toss with desired amount of dressing and feta cheese and serve.

INGREDIENTS

1 tablespoon Dijon mustard

¼ cup plus 1 tablespoon olive oil

3 tablespoons balsamic vinegar

3 tablespoons red wine vinegar

1 pound yellow squash, cut into ½-inch pieces

1 large zucchini, cut into ½-inch pieces

3 cups baby spinach, stemmed

½ cup cherry tomatoes, halved

6 basil leaves, diced

3 mint leaves, diced

⅓ cup feta cheese, crumbled

VARIATION

If you would like to add a little meat to this salad, whip up the Charred Flank Steak (see page 207). Simply season and grill the steak over medium-high heat for about 4 to 5 minutes per side until medium-rare. Slice and mix into the salad before adding the dressing, and serve.

HOUSE SALAD

Makes 6 servings / Active Time: 10 minutes / Total Time: 20 minutes

This basic, hearty salad is a good complement to a large steak or pork chop. For a dash of smokiness, pair this with a side of Charred Scallions (see page 389).

INGREDIENTS

3 heads of preferred lettuce

1 small red onion, sliced into ¼-inch rings

10 Kalamata olives

1 cucumber, sliced

4 cherry tomatoes, halved

1 red bell pepper, seeded and diced

6 pepperoncini peppers

2 garlic cloves, minced

¼ cup red wine vinegar

¾ cup olive oil

Coarsely ground black pepper

Sea salt

¼ cup feta cheese, cubed

1   Rinse the heads of lettuce, dry them thoroughly, and roughly chop. In a medium bowl, combine the lettuce, red onion, Kalamata olives, cucumber, tomatoes, bell pepper, and pepperoncini peppers and set in the refrigerator.

2   In a small jar, whisk together the minced garlic, red wine vinegar, and olive oil, and then season with black pepper and sea salt. Chill in the refrigerator for 15 minutes.

3   Remove the salad and the vinaigrette from the refrigerator, add the pieces of feta, and mix together. Serve immediately.

THE ELEMENTS OF STYLE
RUBS, MARINADES, SAUCES, BUTTERS, BASTES & GLAZES

THE ELEMENTS OF STYLE
RUBS, MARINADES, SAUCES, BUTTERS, BASTES & GLAZES

RUBS

Cooking with rubs requires attention to both the cooking process itself and the end result. Odds are, if you're going to be grilling over a high-temperature flame, you'll want a rub that will be crusted and seared onto the exterior of the meat. On the other hand, if you're using a cast-iron Dutch oven or a slow cooker, you'll want a rub that will hug the meat's exterior while seeping into its body and fats. Whether it adds a unique texture, a crisp char, a burst of heat, or simply emphasizes the juiciness of the meat, a rub is the easiest, as well as the best, way to spice things up and make a recipe your own.

From the many summers I've spent hanging around the firepit, there are a couple small things I've learned about working with rubs. First off, you never want to start with too much rub. When it comes to rubs, you can always add more, but it's impossible to take it back. Operating along those same lines, you never want to use too nice of a cut of meat when figuring out just how much of a rub you'll want. Not only will a good rub elevate a lesser cut of meat, it will save you from sullying that fine porterhouse.

When I first started experimenting with different rubs, I often worked with London broils and whole chickens—meats that are inexpensive and offer a large surface area. You'll always want to keep the surface area in mind; if you're looking to prepare a Steak au Poivre, you're going to want to use a Filet Mignon rather than a London broil—that is, unless you love pepper. You are likely to find that rubs are used to capture the overall mood that you're shooting for. Sometimes, though, you'll find that you'd rather the meat stand on its own with an herbal sauce, such as a chimichurri, on the side.

While you should be prepared to experiment with your rubs, once you find the seasonings that you love, run with them. Mix this with that, learning along the way which flavors are instant classics and which are good for certain occasions. Before you get started, make sure that you have a nice bottle of extra virgin olive oil by your side, as you'll want to apply a very thin layer to the meat before adding the rub.

MARINADES

In general, you'll find that the central ingredient to a successful marinade is time. Most of the marinades that follow don't require too much prep time. Over the past several summers, I've spent many afternoons thinking of the next day's meal, contemplating which meat I'd be purchasing and which marinade I'd be working with. If you work a day job, you'll quickly realize that planning ahead is absolutely necessary when you work with marinades. Having your meat marinating in the refrigerator before you head off to the office is the best way to do it, though there are some meats you may want to marinate through the night.

There really is no such thing as marinating for too long—within reason. Don't start marinating for a week at a time, as your meat will definitely go bad. However, when you see the marinating times for each recipe, understand that this is the low end of the time spectrum. In general, if you have the time, marinate longer. The longer you marinate, the more your meat will take on the desired flavor.

Unlike rubs and sauces, marinades can be a much gentler and delicate recipe-booster. Since most meats don't take on too much of the marinade's flavor unless you're working with a marinade like teriyaki, you have much more room to experiment. Most meats are flexible and forgiving when it comes to marinades, and you'll find that the simplest combinations—such as a red wine-and-rosemary marinade for red meat, or a white wine, thyme, and lemon juice marinade for poultry and seafood—are real crowd-pleasers.

SAUCES

Sauces and gravies make whatever meat is on your grill a memorable meal. With the recipes in this section, you'll discover there's a simple framework for making sauces and gravies. If you add the right ingredients at the right times, you'll have a sauce perfect for whatever you're grilling.

Sauces are structured around one of three foundational components: liquids, vegetables, or herbs. Nearly all liquid-based sauces start with oil, cream, stock, broth, beer, wine, or liquor.

Sauces made from vegetables—such as a tomato sauce—or herbs—such as a chimichurri—don't take long to prepare, and they're compatible with a variety of meats. Ingredients for these sauces are typically either finely chopped and combined in a small bowl with extra virgin olive oil, or pulsed in a food processor while the olive oil is gradually added.

For any sort of gravy, the roux is a necessary component. A white roux is composed of equal parts butter and flour and can either be made ahead of time or added to the sauce toward the end of the cooking process. When making ahead, set a small frying pan over medium heat and add 1 or 2 tablespoons of unsalted butter to the pan. When the butter has melted, stir in an equal amount of flour and beat the mixture until the roux reaches a thick consistency. The roux should not be browned, but it should have a hint of gold in it. Toward the end of the sauce's cooking time, add the roux, then continue to heat for another 1 to 2 minutes until the sauce thickens and becomes a gravy.

BUTTERS, BASTES & GLAZES

Perhaps no barbecue dinner is complete without these. Bastes and glazes essentially serve as a marinade to use during the grilling process. A baste will add wonderful moisture to your meat. If you're short on time, whip up one of the marinades or sauces that follow and generously apply it while your meat is cooking. A glaze will supply the meat with a crisp, glossy layer, and can be achieved by brushing the meat with a vinegar or a sugary component such as honey.

By mixing any of the rubs that follow into a few tablespoons of butter, you can take a meal to the next level. Prepare them well ahead of time, allotting 1 tablespoon for each serving of meat.

SOUTHWESTERN DRY RUB

WORKS BEST WITH:	☑ BEEF	☑ LAMB	☑ PORK
	☑ POULTRY	☐ SEAFOOD	
FLAVOR:	☑ SPICY	☐ SWEET	☐ TANGY
	☑ SAVORY	☑ SALTY	

INGREDIENTS

2 teaspoons chili powder

2 teaspoons paprika

1 teaspoon cayenne pepper

1 teaspoon cumin

1 teaspoon ground coriander

1 teaspoon garlic, minced

1 teaspoon kosher salt

1 teaspoon ground black pepper

Using a spoon, combine all of the ingredients in a small bowl and mix thoroughly. Apply to meat when finished.

VARIATION 1

For more heat, add 1 teaspoon of minced habanero pepper. Be sure to have plenty of bread and milk nearby to balance the spice.

VARIATION 2

For a smokier flavor, consider adding 1 or 2 teaspoons of liquid smoke to the rub. I recommend Colgin's.

RUSTIC PEPPER DRY RUB

WORKS BEST WITH:
- ☑ BEEF
- ☑ POULTRY
- ☑ LAMB
- ☑ SEAFOOD
- ☐ PORK

FLAVOR:
- ☑ SPICY
- ☑ SAVORY
- ☐ SWEET
- ☑ SALTY
- ☐ TANGY

INGREDIENTS

2 garlic cloves, minced

2 teaspoons thyme, minced

2 teaspoons sea salt

1½ teaspoons coarsely ground black pepper

1½ teaspoons coarsely ground white pepper

1 teaspoon coarsely ground red pepper

1 teaspoon sweet paprika

½ teaspoon onion powder

Using a spoon, combine all of the ingredients in a small bowl and mix thoroughly. Apply to meat when finished.

ST. LOUIS RUB

WORKS BEST WITH: ☑ BEEF ☐ LAMB ☑ PORK
☑ POULTRY ☐ SEAFOOD

FLAVOR: ☐ SPICY ☐ SWEET ☐ TANGY
☑ SAVORY ☑ SALTY

INGREDIENTS

¼ cup paprika

3 tablespoons garlic powder

2 tablespoons ground black pepper

2 tablespoons kosher salt

2 tablespoons onion powder

1 tablespoon dark brown sugar

1 tablespoon ground ginger

1 tablespoon mustard powder

1 teaspoon celery salt

Using a spoon, combine all of the ingredients in a small bowl and mix thoroughly. Apply to meat when finished.

VARIATION

For a smokier flavor, consider adding 1 or 2 teaspoons of liquid smoke to the rub. I recommend Colgin's.

YOUR GO-TO STEAK RUB

WORKS BEST WITH:	☑ BEEF	☑ LAMB	☑ PORK
	☐ POULTRY	☐ SEAFOOD	
FLAVOR:	☐ SPICY	☐ SWEET	☐ TANGY
	☑ SAVORY	☐ SALTY	

INGREDIENTS

2 tablespoons ground black pepper

2 tablespoons sweet paprika

3 teaspoons kosher salt

1 tablespoon onion powder

1 tablespoon garlic powder

2 teaspoons ground cumin

Using a spoon, combine all of the ingredients in a small bowl and mix thoroughly. Apply to meat when finished.

SMOKED PAPRIKA RUB

WORKS BEST WITH:	☑ BEEF	☑ LAMB	☑ PORK
	☑ POULTRY	☐ SEAFOOD	
FLAVOR:	☐ SPICY	☐ SWEET	☐ TANGY
	☑ SAVORY	☑ SALTY	

INGREDIENTS

2 tablespoons smoked paprika

2 teaspoons ground coriander

2 teaspoons ground cumin

1 teaspoon cayenne pepper

1 tablespoon coarsely ground black pepper

1 tablespoon sea salt

In a small bowl, thoroughly combine all the ingredients and store at room temperature in a sealed container for up to 1 month.

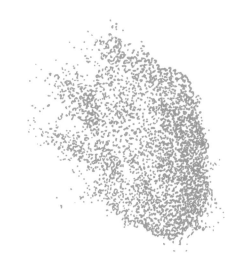

CLASSIC SEAFOOD RUB

WORKS BEST WITH: ☐ BEEF   ☐ LAMB   ☐ PORK
                       ☑ POULTRY   ☑ SEAFOOD

FLAVOR: ☐ SPICY   ☐ SWEET   ☐ TANGY
                  ☑ SAVORY   ☑ SALTY

INGREDIENTS

2 tablespoons sweet paprika

2 tablespoons garlic powder

1 tablespoon dry mustard

1 tablespoon ancho chili powder

1 tablespoon onion powder

1 tablespoon coarsely ground black pepper

1 tablespoon sea salt

1 teaspoon ground cinnamon

1 teaspoon ground cumin

In a small bowl, thoroughly combine all the ingredients and store in an airtight container at room temperature for up to 1 month.

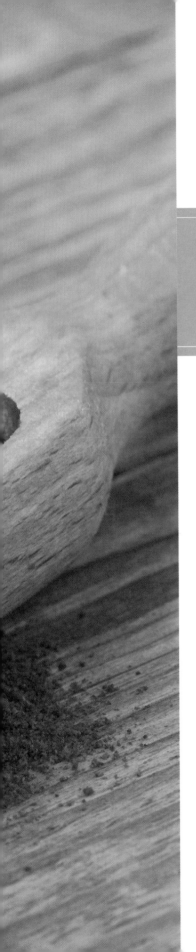

ANCHO CHILI RUB

WORKS BEST WITH:	☑ BEEF	☐ LAMB	☑ PORK
	☑ POULTRY	☐ SEAFOOD	
FLAVOR:	☑ SPICY	☑ SWEET	☐ TANGY
	☑ SAVORY	☐ SALTY	

INGREDIENTS

2 tablespoons sweet paprika

1 tablespoon ancho chili powder

1 tablespoon ground coriander

1 tablespoon ground cumin

2 teaspoons dried oregano

1 tablespoon ground allspice

1 teaspoon onion powder

½ teaspoon cinnamon

In a small bowl, mix together all the ingredients and store at room temperature for up to 1 month.

NOTE: *Although you may think that this is a very hot rub, it is actually fairly mild. Unlike regular chili powder, ancho chili powder comes from the ancho chili pepper, which is actually relatively sweet. As such, I paired the sweetness of the ancho chili powder with the sweetness of the paprika.*

CAJUN RUB

WORKS BEST WITH:	☑ BEEF	☑ LAMB	☑ PORK
	☑ POULTRY	☑ SEAFOOD	
FLAVOR:	☐ SPICY	☐ SWEET	☐ TANGY
	☑ SAVORY	☑ SALTY	

INGREDIENTS

¼ cup sea salt

2 tablespoons ground black pepper

2 teaspoons paprika

2 teaspoons garlic powder

1 teaspoon onion powder

1 teaspoon cayenne pepper

1 teaspoon thyme, minced

Using a spoon, combine all of the ingredients in a small bowl and mix thoroughly. Apply to meat when finished.

VARIATION

For a smokier flavor, consider adding 1 or 2 teaspoons of liquid smoke to the rub. I recommend Colgin's.

HERBAL RUB

WORKS BEST WITH: ☑ BEEF ☑ LAMB ☐ PORK
☑ POULTRY ☑ SEAFOOD

FLAVOR: ☐ SPICY ☐ SWEET ☐ TANGY
☑ SAVORY ☑ SALTY

INGREDIENTS

¼ cup fresh flat-leaf parsley, minced

¼ cup fresh rosemary, minced

4 to 6 medium garlic cloves, diced

1 tablespoon coarsely ground black pepper

2 tablespoons sea salt

¼ cup extra virgin olive oil

1 In a small bowl, thoroughly combine the parsley, rosemary, garlic, black pepper, and sea salt.

2 Slowly whisk in ¼ cup of olive oil until ingredients form into a smooth paste.

3 Let the rub stand at room temperature for 30 minutes before applying to the meat.

VARIATION

If you would like to turn this into a marinade for a rib roast or other large piece of red meat, increase the amount of extra virgin olive oil to 1¼ cups. Transfer the marinade into a large bowl, followed by the meat. Note that the meat will most likely not be completely submerged in the marinade, so be sure to constantly shift the meat so that all sides receive equal marinating times. Let the meat marinate for 1 hour.

COFFEE RUB

WORKS BEST WITH: ☑ **BEEF**   ☐ **LAMB**   ☑ **PORK**
   ☑ **POULTRY**   ☐ **SEAFOOD**

FLAVOR: ☐ **SPICY**   ☑ **SWEET**   ☑ **TANGY**
   ☑ **SAVORY**   ☐ **SALTY**

INGREDIENTS

¼ cup ground coffee

2 tablespoons dark brown sugar

2 tablespoons cayenne pepper

2 tablespoons garlic powder

2 tablespoons paprika

2 tablespoons onion powder

1 tablespoon ground cumin

1 tablespoon kosher salt

Using a spoon, combine all of the ingredients in a small bowl and mix thoroughly. Apply to meat when finished.

INDIAN CURRY RUB

WORKS BEST WITH:	☐ BEEF	☑ LAMB	☐ PORK
	☑ POULTRY	☑ SEAFOOD	

FLAVOR:	☑ SPICY	☐ SWEET	☐ TANGY
	☐ SAVORY	☐ SALTY	

INGREDIENTS

2 tablespoons yellow curry powder

1 tablespoon smoked paprika

1 tablespoon ground ginger

2 teaspoons ground cumin

2 teaspoons ground allspice

2 teaspoons coarsely ground black pepper

1 teaspoon sea salt

In a small bowl, thoroughly combine all the ingredients for the rub and store in an airtight container at room temperature for up to 1 month.

SMOKED SEAFOOD RUB

WORKS BEST WITH:
☐ BEEF ☐ LAMB ☐ PORK
☑ POULTRY ☑ SEAFOOD

FLAVOR:
☑ SPICY ☐ SWEET ☐ TANGY
☑ SAVORY ☑ SALTY

INGREDIENTS

1 tablespoon paprika

1 tablespoon ground black pepper

1 teaspoon dried basil

1 teaspoon dried tarragon

1 teaspoon garlic, minced

1 teaspoon lemon zest

½ teaspoon chili powder

½ teaspoon onion powder

Using a spoon, combine all of the ingredients in a small bowl and mix thoroughly. Apply to meat when finished.

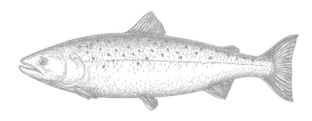

HOT AND SPICY CHILI RUB

WORKS BEST WITH:	☑ BEEF	☑ LAMB	☑ PORK
	☑ POULTRY	☑ SEAFOOD	
FLAVOR:	☑ SPICY	☐ SWEET	☑ TANGY
	☐ SAVORY	☐ SALTY	

INGREDIENTS

3 tablespoons chili powder

3 tablespoons smoked paprika

1 tablespoon dried oregano

2 teaspoons ground cumin

2 teaspoons coarsely ground black pepper

2 teaspoons sea salt

1 teaspoon dried thyme

In a small bowl, thoroughly combine all the ingredients for the rub and store in an airtight container at room temperature for up to 1 month.

DILL AND CORIANDER RUB

WORKS BEST WITH:

☐ BEEF ☑ LAMB ☑ PORK
☑ POULTRY ☐ SEAFOOD

FLAVOR:

☐ SPICY ☐ SWEET ☐ TANGY
☑ SAVORY ☑ SALTY

INGREDIENTS

3 tablespoons coarsely ground black pepper

3 tablespoons coriander seeds

2 tablespoons fresh dill, minced

2 medium garlic cloves, minced

2 tablespoons sea salt

1 Combine all of the ingredients in a medium bowl and whisk together thoroughly.

2 Allow your meat of choice to rest at room temperature for 1 hour before seasoning with the rub.

VARIATION

The Dill and Coriander Rub can be transformed into a marinade for poultry by adding 1 cup of extra virgin olive oil to the rub ingredients.

FINGER-LICKIN' GOOD BBQ RUB

WORKS BEST WITH:
☑ BEEF ☐ LAMB ☑ PORK
☑ POULTRY ☑ SEAFOOD

FLAVOR:
☑ SPICY ☐ SWEET ☑ TANGY
☑ SAVORY ☐ SALTY

INGREDIENTS

¼ cup brown sugar

¼ cup sweet paprika

1 tablespoon onion powder

1 tablespoon dried oregano

1 tablespoon dried savory

3 teaspoons cayenne pepper

2 teaspoons garlic powder

3 tablespoons kosher salt

1 tablespoon coarsely ground black pepper

Combine all of the ingredients in a medium bowl and whisk together thoroughly. Use immediately.

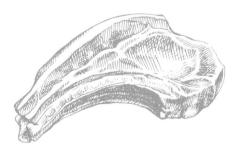

OREGANO-GARLIC RUB

WORKS BEST WITH:	☑ BEEF	☐ LAMB	☑ PORK
	☑ POULTRY	☑ SEAFOOD	
FLAVOR:	☐ SPICY	☐ SWEET	☐ TANGY
	☑ SAVORY	☑ SALTY	

INGREDIENTS

1 tablespoon fresh oregano, minced

2 garlic cloves, minced

2 sprigs of thyme, leaves removed

2 teaspoons coarsely ground black pepper

1 teaspoon sea salt

1 teaspoon ground cumin

1 teaspoon ground coriander

In a small bowl, thoroughly combine all the ingredients for the rub and store in an airtight container at room temperature for up to 1 week.

NOTE: *Fresh oregano is a must, as dry oregano becomes less potent when it is stored for long periods of time.*

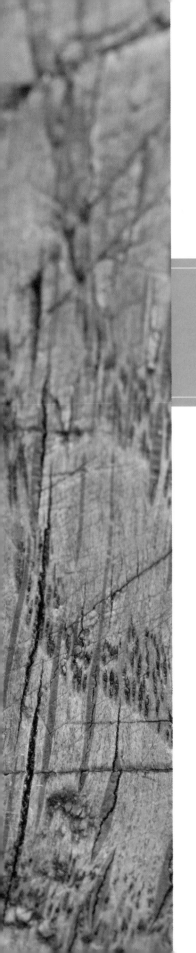

TOASTED FENNEL SEED RUB

WORKS BEST WITH:	☐ BEEF	☐ LAMB	☐ PORK
	☑ POULTRY	☑ SEAFOOD	
FLAVOR:	☐ SPICY	☐ SWEET	☐ TANGY
	☑ SAVORY	☑ SALTY	

TOOLS

Frying pan

INGREDIENTS

¼ cup fennel seeds

1 tablespoon coriander seeds

2 teaspoons whole black peppercorns

2 teaspoons sea salt

1 Place a small frying pan over medium heat and toast the fennel and coriander seeds until they are fragrant, about 1 to 2 minutes. Remove from heat and let cool.

2 When cool, place the seeds and the peppercorns in a small, resealable plastic bag. Using the dull side of the knife, grind the fennel seeds, coriander seeds, and the whole black peppercorns into a rub. Stir in the sea salt and use immediately.

MEDITERRANEAN RUB

WORKS BEST WITH:	☑ BEEF	☑ LAMB	☑ PORK
	☑ POULTRY	☑ SEAFOOD	
FLAVOR:	☐ SPICY	☐ SWEET	☐ TANGY
	☑ SAVORY	☐ SALTY	

INGREDIENTS

2 garlic cloves, minced

2 tablespoons rosemary, minced

1 tablespoon thyme, chopped

1 tablespoon ground black pepper

2 teaspoons sea salt

1 teaspoon lemon zest

Using a spoon, combine all of the ingredients in a small bowl and mix thoroughly. Apply to meat when finished.

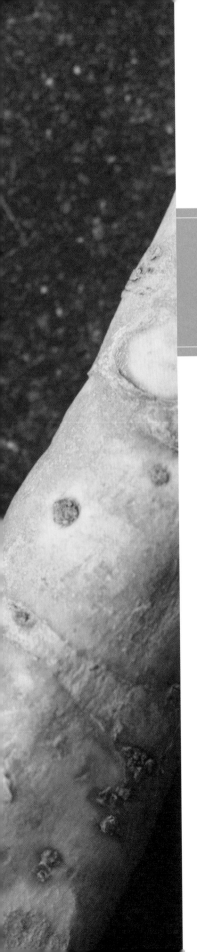

HORSERADISH CRUST

WORKS BEST WITH:	☑ BEEF	☑ LAMB	☑ PORK
	☑ POULTRY	☑ SEAFOOD	
FLAVOR:	☑ SPICY	☐ SWEET	☐ TANGY
	☑ SAVORY	☑ SALTY	

INGREDIENTS

1 stick of unsalted butter, softened

6 garlic cloves

¾ cup horseradish, grated

¼ cup thyme, minced

2 tablespoons rosemary, minced

3 tablespoons coarsely ground black pepper

2 tablespoons sea salt

1   In a small food processor, pulse together the softened butter, garlic, and horseradish. Transfer to a medium bowl.

2   Place the remaining ingredients in the bowl, mash to combine, and then let stand at room temperate for 30 minutes before applying to the meat.

VARIATION

If you would like to use an oil-based crust, substitute ¾ cup extra virgin olive oil for the 1 stick of unsalted butter. If using oil, you can skip the food processor and instead combine all of the ingredients in a medium bowl.

PASTRAMI RUB

WORKS BEST WITH:
- ☑ BEEF
- ☐ POULTRY
- ☐ LAMB
- ☐ SEAFOOD
- ☑ PORK

FLAVOR:
- ☐ SPICY
- ☐ SAVORY
- ☐ SWEET
- ☑ SALTY
- ☐ TANGY

INGREDIENTS

2 tablespoons ground coriander

4 tablespoons ground pepper

1 tablespoon mustard powder

2 tablespoons sea salt

2 teaspoons garlic powder

2 teaspoons onion powder

1 tablespoon dark brown sugar

2 tablespoons paprika

Using a spoon, combine all of the ingredients in a small bowl and mix thoroughly. Apply to meat when finished.

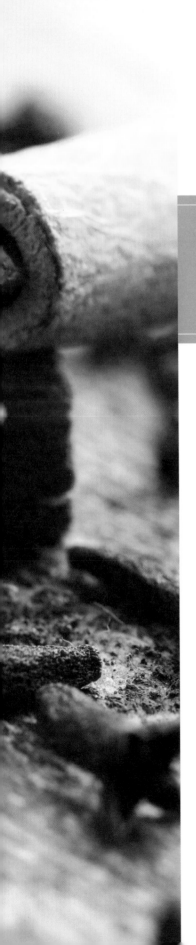

CHINESE FIVE-SPICE RUB

WORKS BEST WITH:	☑ BEEF	☐ LAMB	☑ PORK
	☑ POULTRY	☐ SEAFOOD	
FLAVOR:	☑ SPICY	☐ SWEET	☐ TANGY
	☑ SAVORY	☐ SALTY	

INGREDIENTS

1 tablespoon ground star anise

1 tablespoon ground cinnamon

1 tablespoon ground Sichuan peppercorns

1 tablespoon ground fennel seeds

1 tablespoon ground cloves

1 tablespoon garlic powder

1 tablespoon ground ginger

1 tablespoon sea salt

Using a spoon, combine all of the ingredients in a small bowl and mix thoroughly. Apply to meat when finished.

VARIATION

For more of a kick, try adding half of a finely chopped habanero pepper. Be careful, though, the more seeds you include the hotter it will be!

BARBECUED SHRIMP DRY RUB

WORKS BEST WITH:
- ☐ BEEF
- ☑ POULTRY
- ☐ LAMB
- ☑ SEAFOOD
- ☐ PORK

FLAVOR:
- ☐ SPICY
- ☑ SAVORY
- ☐ SWEET
- ☑ SALTY
- ☐ TANGY

INGREDIENTS

1 tablespoon paprika

1 tablespoon ancho chili powder

1 teaspoon garlic powder

1 tablespoon ground black pepper

1 tablespoon sea salt

1 teaspoon dried oregano

1 teaspoon red pepper flakes

Using a spoon, combine all of the ingredients in a small bowl and mix thoroughly. Apply to meat when finished.

TERIYAKI MARINADE

WORKS BEST WITH:	☑ BEEF	☐ LAMB	☑ PORK
	☑ POULTRY	☐ SEAFOOD	
FLAVOR:	☐ SPICY	☑ SWEET	☐ TANGY
	☑ SAVORY	☑ SALTY	

INGREDIENTS

½ cup soy sauce

¼ cup brown sugar

2 tablespoons rice vinegar

2 garlic cloves, minced

2 teaspoons ginger, minced

1 teaspoon ground black pepper

1 In a bowl, combine all of the ingredients and stir until the sugar has dissolved completely.

2 Apply marinade to meat immediately and marinate for at least 4 hours.

OLIVE OIL AND GARLIC MARINADE

WORKS BEST WITH:	☑ BEEF	☑ LAMB	☑ PORK
	☑ POULTRY	☐ SEAFOOD	
FLAVOR:	☑ SPICY	☐ SWEET	☐ TANGY
	☑ SAVORY	☐ SALTY	

INGREDIENTS

12 garlic cloves, crushed

Leaves from 6 sprigs of rosemary

Leaves from 4 sprigs of thyme

2½ cups extra virgin olive oil

1 tablespoon coarsely ground black pepper

1 tablespoon sea salt

1   Add all of the ingredients to a bowl large enough to hold the meat comfortably. Transfer the marinade to the refrigerator and let stand for about 45 minutes.

2   Place the meat in the marinade and let marinate for 2 hours in the refrigerator. If the meat isn't fully submerged in the marinade, rotate it a couple of times during the marinating process.

3   Remove the meat from the marinade 30 minutes before grilling and place on a roasting rack so that the marinade seeps out of the meat.

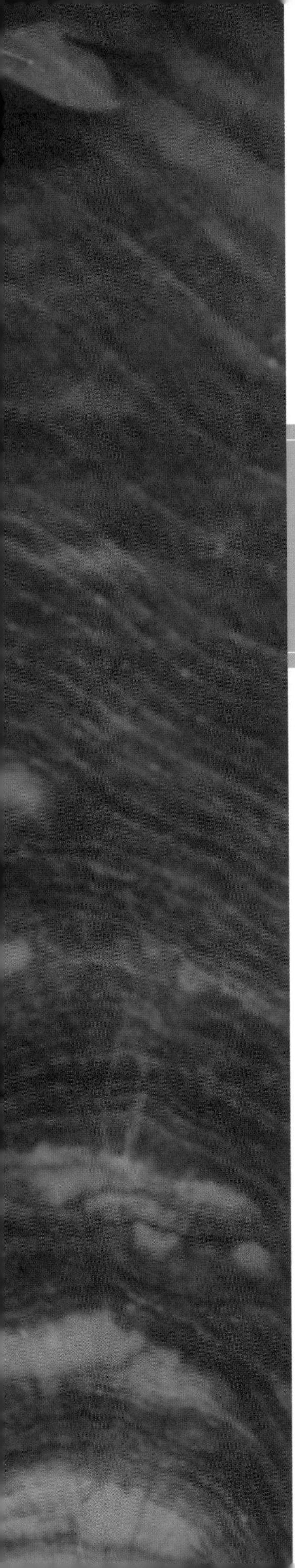

RED WINE AND DIJON MARINADE

WORKS BEST WITH:	☑ BEEF	☑ LAMB	☑ PORK
	☑ POULTRY	☐ SEAFOOD	
FLAVOR:	☑ SPICY	☐ SWEET	☑ TANGY
	☑ SAVORY	☐ SALTY	

INGREDIENTS

¾ cup dry red wine

¼ cup extra virgin olive oil

2 garlic cloves, minced

1 tablespoon Dijon mustard

1 tablespoon coarsely ground black pepper

1 tablespoon sea salt

1 teaspoon rosemary, finely chopped

1   Add all of the ingredients to a large bowl that will be able to hold the meat. Transfer the marinade into the refrigerator and let stand for about 45 minutes.

2   Add the meat to the marinade and let marinate for 2 hours in the refrigerator. If the meat isn't fully submerged in the marinade, rotate it a couple of times during the marinating process.

3   Remove the meat from the marinade 30 minutes before grilling and place on a roasting rack so that the marinade seeps out of the meat.

4   While cooking, baste the meat with the remaining marinade.

APPLE CIDER MARINADE

WORKS BEST WITH:
- ☐ BEEF
- ☑ POULTRY
- ☐ LAMB
- ☐ SEAFOOD
- ☑ PORK

FLAVOR:
- ☐ SPICY
- ☑ SAVORY
- ☑ SWEET
- ☐ SALTY
- ☐ TANGY

INGREDIENTS

2 cups fresh apple cider

¼ cup olive oil

Juice from ½ lemon

Leaves from 2 sprigs of thyme, minced

Leaves from 2 sprigs of rosemary, minced

2 garlic cloves, minced

1 tablespoon coarsely ground black pepper

2 teaspoons sea salt

1   In a medium bowl or roasting pan, combine all the ingredients for the marinade and let rest for 15 minutes.

2   Add your desired meat to the marinade. Transfer to the refrigerator and let marinate from 4 hours to overnight. If the marinade does not fully cover the meat, turn the meat halfway through the marinating process so that all areas of the meat receive equal amounts of the marinade.

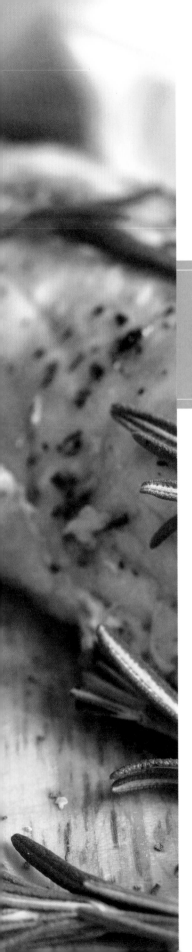

LEMON-ROSEMARY MARINADE

WORKS BEST WITH:	☐ BEEF	☑ LAMB	☑ PORK
	☑ POULTRY	☑ SEAFOOD	
FLAVOR:	☐ SPICY	☐ SWEET	☑ TANGY
	☑ SAVORY	☐ SALTY	

INGREDIENTS

Juice from 4 lemons

6 garlic cloves, minced

Leaves from 3 sprigs of thyme

Leaves from 3 sprigs of rosemary

2 teaspoons ground fennel seeds

1 tablespoon coarsely ground black pepper

1 tablespoon sea salt

1. In a medium bowl, combine all the ingredients and let stand for 15 minutes.

2. Add the meat to the marinade. Transfer to the refrigerator and let marinate for at least 4 hours. If the marinade does not fully cover the meat, turn the meat halfway through the marinating process so that all areas of the meat receive equal amounts of the marinade.

PINEAPPLE MARINADE

WORKS BEST WITH:	☐ BEEF	☐ LAMB	☑ PORK
	☑ POULTRY	☐ SEAFOOD	
FLAVOR:	☐ SPICY	☑ SWEET	☑ TANGY
	☐ SAVORY	☐ SALTY	

INGREDIENTS

1½ cups pineapple juice

¼ cup brown sugar

¼ cup soy sauce

2 garlic cloves, minced

1 teaspoon sea salt

1 In a bowl, combine all of the ingredients and stir until the sugar has dissolved completely.

2 Place meat in marinade and marinate for at least 30 minutes.

BALSAMIC MARINADE

WORKS BEST WITH:	☑ BEEF	☐ LAMB	☑ PORK
	☐ POULTRY	☐ SEAFOOD	
FLAVOR:	☐ SPICY	☑ SWEET	☑ TANGY
	☐ SAVORY	☐ SALTY	

INGREDIENTS

4 basil leaves

Leaves from 2 sprigs of rosemary

2 garlic cloves, crushed

2 teaspoons Dijon mustard

1 teaspoon raw honey

1 cup olive oil

¼ cup balsamic vinegar

1 tablespoon coarsely ground black pepper

1 tablespoon sea salt

1 In a medium bowl or roasting pan, combine all of the marinade ingredients and let stand for 15 minutes.

2 Add your desired meat to the marinade. Transfer to the refrigerator and let marinate from 4 hours to overnight. The marinade may not fully cover the meat. In that case, turn the meat halfway through the marinating process so that all areas of the meat receive equal amounts of the marinade.

MINT MARINADE

WORKS BEST WITH:	☑ BEEF	☑ LAMB	☑ PORK
	☐ POULTRY	☐ SEAFOOD	
FLAVOR:	☐ SPICY	☐ SWEET	☑ TANGY
	☐ SAVORY	☐ SALTY	

INGREDIENTS

½ cup olive oil

½ cup fresh mint leaves, minced

¼ cup dry red wine

4 garlic cloves, minced

1 tablespoon fresh parsley, minced

1 tablespoon coarsely ground black pepper

2 teaspoons sea salt

1 In a medium bowl or roasting pan, combine all of the ingredients and let stand for 15 minutes.

2 Add your desired meat to the marinade. Transfer to the refrigerator and let marinate from 4 hours to overnight. Note that the marinade may not fully cover the meat. In that case, turn the meat halfway through the marinating process so that all areas of the meat receive equal amounts of the marinade.

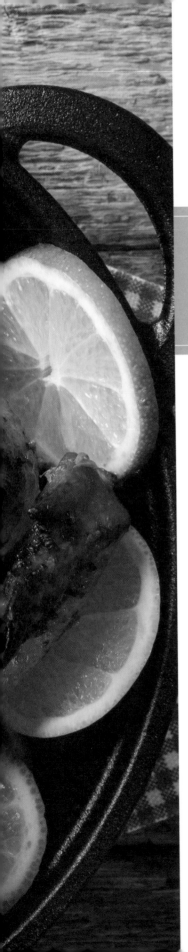

CITRUS MARINADE

WORKS BEST WITH:	☐ BEEF	☐ LAMB	☑ PORK
	☑ POULTRY	☑ SEAFOOD	
FLAVOR:	☐ SPICY	☑ SWEET	☑ TANGY
	☑ SAVORY	☐ SALTY	

INGREDIENTS

¾ cup orange juice

Juice from ½ lime

Juice from ½ lemon

¼ cup cilantro, minced

¼ cup extra virgin olive oil

2 tablespoons rosemary, minced

4 garlic cloves, minced

1 tablespoon coarsely ground black pepper

1 tablespoon sea salt

1 Put all of the ingredients in a bowl large enough to also accommodate the meat.

2 Add the meat to the marinade and let marinate for 2 hours in the refrigerator. The meat will not be fully submerged in the marinade, so be sure to rotate it throughout the marinating process in order for all sides to receive equal marinating time.

3 Remove the meat from the marinade 30 minutes before grilling and place on a roasting rack so that the marinade seeps from the meat. Discard the remaining marinade.

FIVE-SPICE MARINADE

WORKS BEST WITH:	☐ BEEF	☐ LAMB	☐ PORK
	☑ POULTRY	☑ SEAFOOD	
FLAVOR:	☐ SPICY	☐ SWEET	☑ TANGY
	☑ SAVORY	☐ SALTY	

INGREDIENTS

¾ cup soy sauce

¼ cup vinegar

2 tablespoons fresh ginger, minced

2 teaspoons sesame oil

2 teaspoons five-spice powder

¼ cup olive oil

1 teaspoon ground black pepper

1 In a bowl, combine all of the ingredients and stir until the five-spice powder has dissolved completely.

2 Apply marinade to meat immediately and marinate for at least 4 hours. If the marinade does not fully cover the meat, be sure to rotate it throughout the marinating process.

CILANTRO-LIME MARINADE

WORKS BEST WITH:	☑ BEEF	☑ LAMB	☑ PORK
	☑ POULTRY	☑ SEAFOOD	
FLAVOR:	☐ SPICY	☐ SWEET	☑ TANGY
	☑ SAVORY	☑ SALTY	

INGREDIENTS

Juice from 2 limes

¼ cup olive oil

¼ cup fresh cilantro, minced

2 garlic cloves, minced

2 teaspoons coarsely ground black pepper

2 teaspoons sea salt

½ teaspoon organic honey

1   In a medium bowl or roasting pan, combine all of the ingredients and let stand for 15 minutes.

2   Add your desired meat to the marinade. Transfer to the refrigerator and let marinate from 4 hours to overnight. If the marinade does not fully cover the meat, turn the meat halfway through the marinating process so that all areas of the meat receive equal amounts of the marinade.

GINGER-SESAME MARINADE

WORKS BEST WITH:	☐ BEEF	☐ LAMB	☑ PORK
	☑ POULTRY	☐ SEAFOOD	
FLAVOR:	☐ SPICY	☐ SWEET	☑ TANGY
	☑ SAVORY	☐ SALTY	

INGREDIENTS

½ cup soy sauce

1 tablespoon fresh ginger, grated

1 tablespoon sesame oil

2 teaspoons sesame seeds

4 scallions, chopped

1 teaspoon ground black pepper

Put all of the ingredients in a bowl large enough to also accommodate the meat. Evenly coat the meat and prepare immediately.

NOTE: *If you know that one of your guests is vegetarian, this particular marinade works wonders with tofu.*

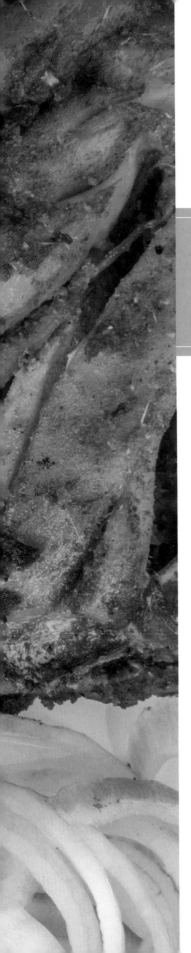

TANDOORI MARINADE

TOOLS

Skillet

INGREDIENTS

2 tablespoons olive oil, plus more as needed

2 garlic cloves, minced

½ teaspoon ground turmeric

2 tablespoons cumin powder

1 tablespoon fresh ginger, minced

1 teaspoon paprika

1 teaspoon coriander seeds

3 tablespoons cilantro, minced

Juice from ½ small lime

1½ cups plain yogurt

1 In a small skillet, heat the olive oil over medium heat. Add everything aside from the lime juice and yogurt to the skillet and toast for 2 minutes. The spices and olive oil should form a paste. If not, add more olive oil to the mixture.

2 Transfer the paste to a bowl and stir in the lime juice and yogurt. Place your meat in the marinade for at least 3 hours before grilling, making sure to rotate the meat at least once while marinating to ensure that it is evenly coated.

ADOBO MARINADE

WORKS BEST WITH:	☑ BEEF	☑ LAMB	☑ PORK
	☑ POULTRY	☑ SEAFOOD	
FLAVOR:	☑ SPICY	☐ SWEET	☐ TANGY
	☑ SAVORY	☑ SALTY	

INGREDIENTS

1 (7 oz.) can of chipotle peppers in adobo

2 garlic cloves, minced

Juice from ½ small lime

1 teaspoon ground black pepper

1 teaspoon sea salt

Add all of the ingredients to a blender and pulse to desired consistency. Remove and marinate meat immediately for as long as desired, making sure to rotate the meat at least once to ensure it is evenly marinated.

JAMAICAN JERK MARINADE

WORKS BEST WITH:	☑ BEEF	☑ LAMB	☑ PORK
	☑ POULTRY	☐ SEAFOOD	
FLAVOR:	☑ SPICY	☐ SWEET	☐ TANGY
	☑ SAVORY	☐ SALTY	

INGREDIENTS

1 medium onion, minced

¼ cup scallions, minced

1 scotch bonnet pepper, chopped

3 tablespoons soy sauce

1 tablespoon white vinegar

3 tablespoons olive oil

2 teaspoons thyme leaves, chopped

2 teaspoons sugar

1 teaspoon sea salt

1 teaspoon ground black pepper

1 teaspoon allspice

½ teaspoon nutmeg

½ teaspoon cinnamon

Place all of the ingredients in a blender and pulse to desired consistency. Remove and marinate meat immediately, making sure to turn at least once to ensure the meat is evenly marinated.

VARIATION

For a smokier version, consider adding 1 or 2 teaspoons of liquid smoke to the marinade. I recommend Colgin's.

STEAK MARINADE

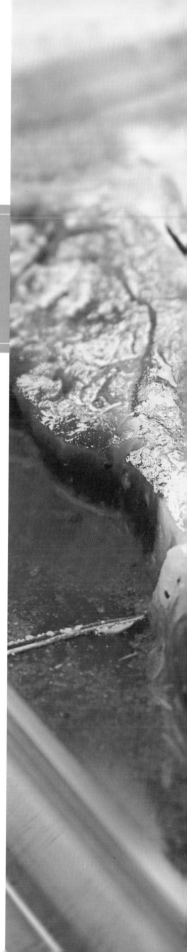

WORKS BEST WITH:	☑ BEEF	☑ LAMB	☐ PORK
	☑ POULTRY	☐ SEAFOOD	
FLAVOR:	☐ SPICY	☐ SWEET	☐ TANGY
	☑ SAVORY	☑ SALTY	

INGREDIENTS

4 garlic cloves, minced

1 tablespoon Dijon mustard

1 tablespoon soy sauce

1 tablespoon olive oil

1 tablespoon Worcestershire sauce

2 teaspoons ground black pepper

1 teaspoon sea salt

1   In a bowl, combine all of the ingredients and stir until the desired consistency has been reached.

2   Marinate the meat for at least 1 hour, rotating halfway through to ensure the meat is evenly marinated.

VARIATION

For a smokier flavor, consider adding 1 or 2 teaspoons of liquid smoke to the marinade. I recommend Colgin's.

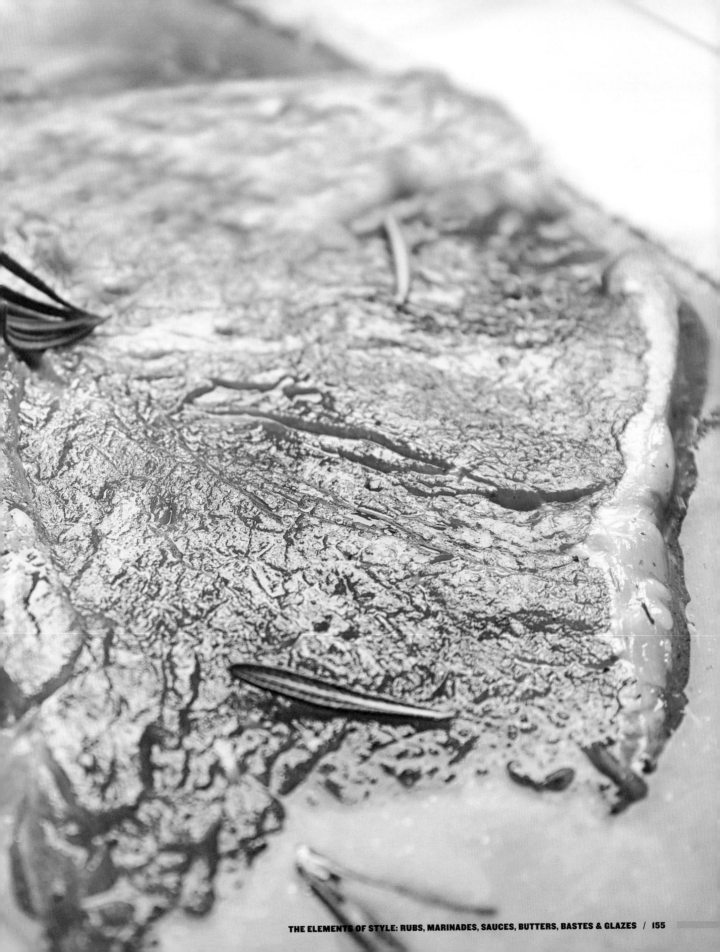

CARNE ASADA MARINADE

WORKS BEST WITH:	☑ BEEF	☑ LAMB	☑ PORK
	☑ POULTRY	☑ SEAFOOD	
FLAVOR:	☑ SPICY	☐ SWEET	☐ TANGY
	☑ SAVORY	☐ SALTY	

INGREDIENTS

Juice from 2 limes

4 garlic cloves, minced

¾ cup orange juice

1 cup cilantro, chopped

1 tablespoon soy sauce

1 teaspoon ground coriander

1 tablespoon sea salt

1 tablespoon ground black pepper

¼ cup olive oil

1   In a bowl, combine all of the ingredients and stir until the desired consistency has been achieved.

2   Marinate meat for at least 1 hour, rotating halfway through to ensure the meat is evenly marinated.

10-MINUTE ALL-PURPOSE MARINADE

WORKS BEST WITH:	☑ BEEF	☑ LAMB	☑ PORK
	☑ POULTRY	☑ SEAFOOD	
FLAVOR:	☐ SPICY	☐ SWEET	☐ TANGY
	☑ SAVORY	☐ SALTY	

INGREDIENTS

½ cup soy sauce

2 tablespoons Worcestershire sauce

2 garlic cloves, minced

¼ medium onion, minced

¼ cup olive oil

Juice from ½ lime

1   In a bowl, combine all of the ingredients and stir until the desired consistency has been achieved.

2   Marinate meat for at least 1 hour, rotating halfway through to ensure the meat is evenly marinated.

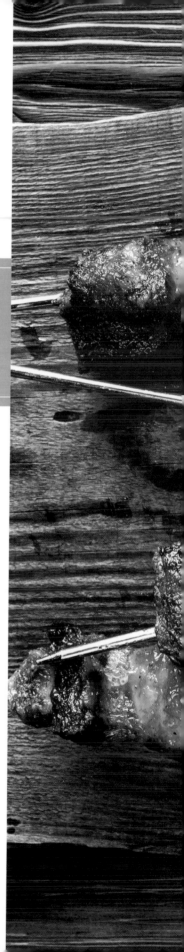

SIMPLE POULTRY BRINE

WORKS BEST WITH:	☐ BEEF	☐ LAMB	☐ PORK
	☑ POULTRY	☐ SEAFOOD	
FLAVOR:	☐ SPICY	☐ SWEET	☐ TANGY
	☐ SAVORY	☑ SALTY	

INGREDIENTS

1 gallon warm water (100°F)

1 cup sea salt

1 cup light brown sugar

¼ cup olive oil

Juice from ½ small lemon

4 garlic cloves, crushed

1 tablespoon ground black pepper

1   In a deep pot, combine all of the ingredients and stir until the desired consistency has been achieved.

2   Add your poultry to the pot and let marinate at room temperature for 2 to 3 hours.

BASIC PORK BRINE

WORKS BEST WITH:	☐ BEEF	☐ LAMB	☑ PORK
	☐ POULTRY	☐ SEAFOOD	
FLAVOR:	☐ SPICY	☐ SWEET	☐ TANGY
	☐ SAVORY	☑ SALTY	

INGREDIENTS

1 gallon warm water (100°F)

¼ cup apple cider vinegar

¼ cup light brown sugar

1 teaspoon thyme, minced

5 garlic cloves, minced

Juice from ½ small lemon

1 tablespoon ground black pepper

2 tablespoons sea salt

1   In a deep pot, combine all of the ingredients and stir until the desired consistency has been achieved.

2   Add your pork to the pot and let marinate at room temperature for 2 to 3 hours.

TOOLS

2 to 3 cups hickory or
oak wood chips

Frying pan

Saucepan

Smoker box (for gas grill)

INGREDIENTS

2 garlic cloves, minced

1 white onion, minced

1½ cups canned crushed tomatoes

½ cup tomato paste

¼ cup white wine vinegar

¼ cup balsamic vinegar

2 tablespoons Dijon mustard

Juice from 1 lime

2 tablespoons ginger, minced

1 teaspoon smoked paprika

½ teaspoon ground cinnamon

2 dried chipotle peppers, minced

1 habanero pepper, seeded and
minced (optional)

1 cup water

Coarsely ground black pepper

Sea salt

SMOKED SOUTHERN BBQ SAUCE

Makes 6 to 8 servings / Active Time: 35 minutes / Total Time: 55 minutes

WORKS BEST WITH:	☑ BEEF	☑ LAMB	☑ PORK	☑ POULTRY	☐ SEAFOOD
FLAVOR:	☑ SPICY	☐ SWEET	☐ TANGY	☑ SAVORY	☑ SALTY
CONSISTENCY:	☐ COARSE	☑ COATING	☐ POURING		

This sauce is filled with intense spice and goes great when served on or alongside barbecued beef and pork dishes, such as the Blackened Texas Brisket with Coleslaw (see pages 230–31).

1 An hour before grilling, place the wood chips in a bowl of water and let them soak.

2 Bring your gas or charcoal grill to medium-high heat.

3 While waiting for the grill to heat up, place a small frying pan over medium heat and, once hot, add the garlic and onion and cook until the garlic has browned and the onion is translucent. Remove from heat and set aside.

4 Transfer the cooked garlic and onion to a food processor with the tomatoes and tomato paste. Puree into a thick paste, and then add the remaining ingredients to the food processor and blend thoroughly. Transfer the sauce to a medium saucepan and set it near the grill.

5 Once the grill is ready, about 425°F with the coals lightly covered with ash, drain 1 cup of the soaked wood chips and spread over the coals or pour into a smoker box. Place the medium saucepan on the grill and then bring the sauce to a boil with the grill covered, aligning the air vent away from the wood chips so that the smoke billows around the sauce before escaping. Let the sauce cook for about 30 to 45 minutes, adding another cup of drained wood chips every 20 minutes until the sauce has reduced to about 2 cups.

6 Remove the sauce from the heat and use immediately. The sauce can be kept refrigerated in an airtight container for up to 2 weeks.

NOTE: *Omit the habanero pepper if you don't like your barbecue sauce on the spicy side.*

MAPLE BBQ SAUCE

Makes 6 to 8 servings / Active Time: 10 minutes / Total Time: 1 hour and 20 minutes

WORKS BEST WITH:	☑ BEEF	☑ LAMB	☑ PORK	☑ POULTRY	☐ SEAFOOD
FLAVOR:	☑ SPICY	☑ SWEET	☐ TANGY	☑ SAVORY	☐ SALTY
CONSISTENCY:	☐ COARSE	☑ COATING	☐ POURING		

The sweetness of the maple syrup works well with all pork recipes. This recipe is also great as a basting sauce for ribs.

1 Place a medium saucepan over medium-high heat. Once hot, add in the onion and garlic and cook until the onion is translucent and the garlic is golden but not browned, about 1 to 2 minutes.

2 Add the remaining ingredients and bring to a boil.

3 Reduce the sauce to a simmer and then cook for about 20 minutes.

4 When the sauce has reduced to about 2 cups, remove from heat and refrigerate for 1 hour before using.

TOOLS

Saucepan

INGREDIENTS

¼ small white onion, minced

2 garlic cloves, minced

1 cup ketchup

3 tablespoons apple cider vinegar

1 tablespoon butter, clarified

½ cup organic maple syrup

2 tablespoons organic molasses

2 teaspoons ground mustard

Coarsely ground black pepper

Sea salt

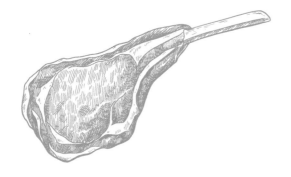

APPLE-MUSTARD BBQ SAUCE

Makes 6 to 8 servings / Active Time: 5 minutes / Total Time: 1 hour

WORKS BEST WITH:	☐ BEEF	☑ LAMB	☑ PORK	☑ POULTRY	☐ SEAFOOD
FLAVOR:	☐ SPICY	☑ SWEET	☐ TANGY	☑ SAVORY	☐ SALTY
CONSISTENCY:	☐ COARSE	☑ COATING	☑ POURING		

Fans of barbecued lamb would do well to try their hand at this smoky and sweet sauce.

Combine all of the ingredients in a small bowl and refrigerate for 1 hour before applying to the meat.

INGREDIENTS

1 tablespoon olive oil

¼ small shallot, minced

¼ cup apple cider

¼ cup white wine vinegar

1 tablespoon tequila

2 teaspoons fresh parsley, minced

3 tablespoons fish sauce

1 tablespoon raw honey

1 tablespoon Dijon mustard

2 teaspoons hot Chinese mustard

Coarsely ground black pepper

Sea salt

BASIL PESTO

Makes 6 to 8 servings / Active Time: 15 minutes / Total Time: 20 minutes

WORKS BEST WITH:	☑ BEEF	☑ LAMB	☑ PORK	☑ POULTRY	☑ SEAFOOD
FLAVOR:	☐ SPICY	☐ SWEET	☐ TANGY	☑ SAVORY	☐ SALTY
CONSISTENCY:	☑ COARSE	☐ COATING	☐ POURING		

Pesto is rooted in herbs and pine nuts—two distinct, savory ingredients that can help almost any meal. Use this as a sauce on pasta, as a crust for a rib roast, or as a topping on a baked potato.

1 Add 2 teaspoons of the olive oil to a small frying pan and place over medium heat. Once hot, add the pine nuts and toast for 1 to 2 minutes until golden but not browned. Remove from heat and transfer to a small cup.

2 In a small food processor, pulse the pine nuts, basil leaves, shallot, and garlic into a thick paste. Next, slowly incorporate the remaining olive oil into until you reach the desired consistency.

3 Using a spatula, remove the pesto from the processor and place in a medium bowl. With a spoon, mix in the Parmesan cheese and then season with the black pepper and sea salt. Serve at room temperature or slightly chilled.

VARIATION

If you want a coarser pesto—or don't have a food processor—you can always use a chef's knife and cutting board to chop the ingredients. In a small bowl, combine the ingredients, then let the pesto marinate for 1 hour before serving.

TOOLS

Frying pan

Food processor

INGREDIENTS

⅓ cup plus 2 teaspoons extra virgin olive oil

⅓ cup pine nuts

3 cups basil leaves

¼ small shallot

2 garlic cloves

¼ cup Parmesan cheese, grated

Coarsely ground black pepper

Sea salt

SUN-DRIED TOMATO PESTO

Makes 6 to 8 servings / Active Time: 10 minutes / Total Time: 15 minutes

WORKS BEST WITH:	☑ BEEF	☑ LAMB	☑ PORK	☑ POULTRY	☑ SEAFOOD
FLAVOR:	☐ SPICY	☐ SWEET	☐ TANGY	☑ SAVORY	☐ SALTY
CONSISTENCY:	☑ COARSE	☐ COATING	☐ POURING		

This sauce is incredibly easy to make—all you need is a food processor, or just a chef's knife, a cutting board, and a small bowl to hold everything!

1 In a small food processor, combine all the ingredients except the extra virgin olive oil and pulse into a thick mixture.

2 Slowly add the extra virgin olive oil and process until your desired consistency is achieved. Serve at room temperature or slightly chilled.

VARIATION

If you want a coarser pesto—or don't have a food processor— you can always use a chef's knife and cutting board to chop the ingredients. In a small bowl, combine them, and then let the pesto marinate for 1 hour before serving.

NOTE: *Serve Sun-Dried Tomato Pesto alongside grilled steaks for added zest.*

TOOLS

Food processor

INGREDIENTS

12 sun-dried tomatoes

½ cup basil leaves

¼ small shallot

¼ cup pine nuts

1 garlic clove

1 tablespoon coarsely ground black pepper

1 teaspoon sea salt

½ cup extra virgin olive oil

GARLIC AND CHIVE STEAK SAUCE

Makes 6 to 8 servings / Active Time: 5 minutes / Total Time: 5 minutes

WORKS BEST WITH:	☑ BEEF	☑ LAMB	☐ PORK	☑ POULTRY	☑ SEAFOOD
FLAVOR:	☑ SPICY	☐ SWEET	☑ TANGY	☐ SAVORY	☐ SALTY
CONSISTENCY:	☑ COARSE	☐ COATING	☐ POURING		

If you're one of those who think this sauce is better suited to a baked potato, you're in for a tremendous surprise.

1   In a small bowl, whisk together the sour cream, chives, garlic, and lemon juice, and then season the sauce with black pepper and sea salt.

2   Store in the refrigerator for up to 3 days and serve at room temperature.

INGREDIENTS

½ cup sour cream

¼ cup fresh chives, minced

3 garlic cloves, minced

Juice from ¼ small lemon

Coarsely ground black pepper

Sea salt

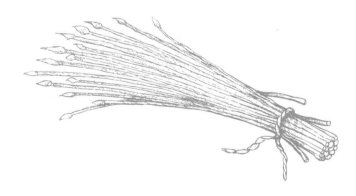

KANSAS CITY BBQ SAUCE

Makes 5 cups / Active Time: 10 minutes / Total Time: 40 minutes

WORKS BEST WITH:	☑ BEEF	☑ LAMB	☑ PORK	☑ POULTRY	☑ SEAFOOD
FLAVOR:	☐ SPICY	☐ SWEET	☐ TANGY	☑ SAVORY	☐ SALTY
CONSISTENCY:	☑ COARSE	☐ COATING	☐ POURING		

BBQ is a major source of regional pride, and this sauce makes it easy to understand why the folks in Kansas City believe their version to be the best.

1 Heat the olive oil in a saucepan over medium heat. Add the minced garlic cloves and cook until golden, about 2 minutes.

2 Stir the remaining ingredients into the saucepan and bring to a simmer. Cover the saucepan and cook until the sauce has been reduced by half, roughly 25 minutes. Make sure to stir the sauce occasionally.

3 When the sauce has been reduced by half, remove from heat, discard the bay leaf, and let stand for 10 minutes before using.

VARIATION

For additional kick, try adding half of a minced habanero pepper. Be careful, though, the more seeds you add the hotter it will become.

TOOLS

Saucepan

INGREDIENTS

2 tablespoons olive oil

4 garlic cloves, minced

2 cups ketchup

1 cup water

¼ cup molasses

¼ cup dark brown sugar

¼ cup apple cider vinegar

2 tablespoons Worcestershire sauce

1 bay leaf

1 teaspoon mustard powder

1 teaspoon chili powder

1 teaspoon onion powder

2 teaspoons liquid smoke

1 teaspoon ground black pepper

1 teaspoon sea salt

SOUTH CAROLINA BBQ SAUCE

Makes 2 cups / Active Time: 10 minutes / Total Time: 1 hour

WORKS BEST WITH:	☑ BEEF	☑ LAMB	☑ PORK	☑ POULTRY	☑ SEAFOOD
FLAVOR:	☐ SPICY	☐ SWEET	☐ TANGY	☑ SAVORY	☐ SALTY
CONSISTENCY:	☑ COARSE	☑ COATING	☐ POURING		

The mustard adds a lovely tangy quality to this sauce, ensuring that its flavor lingers in the mind long after the meal is done.

In a bowl, combine all of the ingredients and let chill for 1 hour in the refrigerator before using.

INGREDIENTS

¾ cup yellow mustard

¼ cup honey

¼ cup apple cider vinegar

1 tablespoon ketchup

1 tablespoon light brown sugar

2 teaspoons Worcestershire sauce

3 garlic cloves, minced

1 teaspoon ground black pepper

PEACH BBQ SAUCE

Makes 4 cups / **Active Time: 15 minutes** / **Total Time: 30 minutes**

WORKS BEST WITH:	☑ BEEF	☑ LAMB	☐ PORK	☑ POULTRY	☑ SEAFOOD
FLAVOR:	☑ SPICY	☐ SWEET	☑ TANGY	☐ SAVORY	☐ SALTY
CONSISTENCY:	☑ COARSE	☑ COATING	☐ POURING		

The sweetness of peaches may seem out of place on your grill, but it's a wonderful complement to the resulting char.

1 Heat the olive oil in a saucepan over medium heat. Add the minced garlic and onion to the saucepan and cook until golden, about 2 minutes.

2 Stir the remaining ingredients into the saucepan and bring to a simmer. Then, cover the saucepan and cook until the sauce has been reduced by half, roughly 10 to 15 minutes, while stirring occasionally.

3 Once the sauce has been reduced, remove from heat and let stand for 10 minutes before using.

TOOLS

Saucepan

INGREDIENTS

2 tablespoons olive oil

4 garlic cloves, minced

1 small onion, minced

1 cup tomatoes, pureed

½ cup ketchup

¼ cup light brown sugar

¼ cup molasses

2 tablespoons honey

1 tablespoon Worcestershire sauce

4 peaches, peeled, pitted, and chopped

2 tablespoons peach preserves

Juice from ½ small lemon

1 teaspoon ground black pepper

1 teaspoon sea salt

ST. LOUIS BBQ SAUCE

Makes 4 cups / Active Time: 20 minutes / Total Time: 1 hour and 15 minutes

WORKS BEST WITH:	☑ BEEF	☑ LAMB	☑ PORK	☑ POULTRY	☑ SEAFOOD
FLAVOR:	☐ SPICY	☐ SWEET	☐ TANGY	☑ SAVORY	☐ SALTY
CONSISTENCY:	☑ COARSE	☑ COATING	☐ POURING		

The molasses, brown sugar, and apple cider vinegar combine to make a rich sauce that brings out the best in everything it touches.

1 Combine all ingredients in a saucepan and place over medium-high heat. Bring the sauce to a boil and cover. Let the sauce boil for 6 minutes.

2 Reduce the heat to low and cook for about 1 hour, stirring occasionally, until the sauce has thickened and been reduced by half.

3 Remove from heat and let stand for 10 minutes before using.

TOOLS

Saucepan

INGREDIENTS

1 (14 oz.) can of pureed tomatoes

2 tablespoons Dijon mustard

¼ cup apple cider vinegar

¼ cup molasses

1 cup dark brown sugar

1 teaspoon Worcestershire sauce

2 garlic cloves, minced

1 teaspoon ground black pepper

1 teaspoon sea salt

HONEY-BOURBON BBQ SAUCE

Makes 3 cups / Active Time: 8 minutes / Total Time: 20 minutes

WORKS BEST WITH:	☑ BEEF	☑ LAMB	☑ PORK	☑ POULTRY	☑ SEAFOOD
FLAVOR:	☐ SPICY	☐ SWEET	☐ TANGY	☑ SAVORY	☐ SALTY
CONSISTENCY:	☑ COARSE	☑ COATING	☐ POURING		

The notes of caramel and vanilla that bourbon is famous for give this sauce considerable depth.

1   Heat the olive oil in a saucepan over medium heat. Add the garlic cloves and cook until golden, about 2 minutes.

2   Stir in the remaining ingredients and bring to a boil. Reduce the heat immediately, cover, and cook for about 6 minutes, or until the sauce has been reduced by about half.

3   Remove from heat and let stand for 10 minutes before using.

TOOLS

Saucepan

INGREDIENTS

2 tablespoons olive oil

4 garlic cloves, minced

1 cup ketchup

½ cup bourbon

3 tablespoons honey

2 tablespoons brown sugar

1 tablespoon soy sauce

1 tablespoon Worcestershire sauce

1 tablespoon Dijon mustard

1 teaspoon liquid smoke

1 teaspoon ground black pepper

1 teaspoon sea salt

MISO BBQ SAUCE

Makes 2 cups / Active Time: 5 minutes / Total Time: 5 minutes

WORKS BEST WITH:	☑ BEEF	☑ LAMB	☑ PORK	☑ POULTRY	☑ SEAFOOD
FLAVOR:	☑ SPICY	☐ SWEET	☑ TANGY	☐ SAVORY	☐ SALTY
CONSISTENCY:	☑ COARSE	☑ COATING	☐ POURING		

The salty, earthy flavor of miso shines in this sauce, which is especially delightful over chicken or grilled shrimp.

In a bowl, use a fork to combine all of the ingredients and stir until the desired consistency has been reached.

INGREDIENTS

3 tablespoons red or white miso

2 tablespoons water

2 garlic cloves, minced

3 tablespoons dark brown sugar

3 tablespoons white vinegar

2 tablespoons ketchup

1 teaspoon ground black pepper

1 teaspoon sea salt

KOREAN BBQ SAUCE

Makes 3 cups / Active Time: 15 minutes / Total Time: 35 minutes

WORKS BEST WITH:	☑ BEEF	☑ LAMB	☑ PORK	☑ POULTRY	☑ SEAFOOD
FLAVOR:	☐ SPICY	☐ SWEET	☐ TANGY	☑ SAVORY	☐ SALTY
CONSISTENCY:	☑ COARSE	☑ COATING	☐ POURING		

Seek out another sauce if you aren't able to find gochujang, as there is no substitute for its flavor.

1 Place a small saucepan over medium heat.

2 Add the soy sauce, ketchup, rice wine vinegar, light brown sugar, gochujang, and garlic to the saucepan and stir until thoroughly combined. Bring to a simmer, cover the saucepan, and let simmer for 15 to 20 minutes, until the sauce has reduced by half.

3 Stir in the remaining ingredients, cook for 2 more minutes, and remove from heat.

4 Let the sauce stand for 10 minutes before using.

TOOLS

Saucepan

INGREDIENTS

½ cup soy sauce

¼ cup ketchup

¼ cup rice wine vinegar

3 tablespoons light brown sugar

1 teaspoon gochujang
(red chili paste)

2 garlic cloves, minced

1 teaspoon sesame oil

1 teaspoon ginger, grated

4 scallions, chopped

1 teaspoon coarsely ground
black pepper

SMOKY STOUT BBQ SAUCE

Makes 3 cups / Active Time: 15 minutes / Total Time: 30 minutes

WORKS BEST WITH: ☑ BEEF ☑ LAMB ☑ PORK ☑ POULTRY ☑ SEAFOOD

FLAVOR: ☐ SPICY ☐ SWEET ☐ TANGY ☑ SAVORY ☐ SALTY

CONSISTENCY: ☑ COARSE ☑ COATING ☐ POURING

Stout has a bitter, chocolaty quality that can work well with a surprising number of grilled meats.

1 Place a small saucepan over medium heat and add all of the ingredients. Bring to a boil, reduce heat, and let simmer for roughly 20 minutes, until the sauce has reduced by a third.

2 Remove from heat and let stand for 10 minutes before using.

TOOLS

Saucepan

INGREDIENTS

1 cup stout beer

1 cup ketchup

½ cup apple cider vinegar

½ cup dark brown sugar

2 tablespoons honey

2 tablespoons Worcestershire sauce

1 teaspoon liquid smoke

1 teaspoon coarsely ground black pepper

1 teaspoon sea salt

UNIVERSAL BBQ SAUCE

Makes 3 cups / Active Time: 10 minutes / Total Time: 15 minutes

WORKS BEST WITH:	☑ BEEF	☑ LAMB	☑ PORK	☑ POULTRY	☑ SEAFOOD
FLAVOR:	☐ SPICY	☑ SWEET	☐ TANGY	☑ SAVORY	☐ SALTY
CONSISTENCY:	☐ COARSE	☑ COATING	☐ POURING		

Looking for a sauce that is certain to satisfy everyone? This delicious version has you covered, taking a little bit of the best from a variety of sauces.

1   In a medium saucepan, combine the ketchup, brown sugar, molasses, apple cider vinegar, water, and Worcestershire sauce and set over medium heat. Whisk in the ground mustard, garlic powder, smoked paprika, and cayenne pepper and bring to a boil. Reduce the heat and let simmer.

2   While the sauce simmers, whisk in the flour. The key is to do this very slowly so that you prevent clumps from forming in the sauce. If clumps do form, add an extra 1 or 2 tablespoons of water to the pot.

3   Let the sauce simmer for about 5 to 7 minutes, and then remove from heat and season with black pepper and sea salt.

TOOLS

Saucepan

INGREDIENTS

1¼ cups ketchup

1 cup dark brown sugar

¼ cup molasses

¼ cup apple cider vinegar

¼ cup water, plus more as needed

1 tablespoon Worcestershire sauce

2 teaspoons ground mustard

2 teaspoons garlic powder

2 teaspoons smoked paprika

¼ teaspoon cayenne pepper

2 tablespoons all-purpose flour

Coarsely ground black pepper

Sea salt

BEEF

BEEF

PERHAPS NO OTHER TYPE OF MEAT is more associated with grilling than beef. After all, beef is our go-to when it comes to flame and hot coals—what's more primal than that?

This past summer, a fortuitous mistake allowed my father and I to explore a whole new level of grilling beef.

We had come home with two beautifully cut porterhouse steaks when we realized we had overlooked a critical component to our big dinner—a grill! We had just moved into our newly renovated home, a 1755 farmhouse along the coast of Maine, and our Weber gas and charcoal grills were both out of commission. We did have plenty of seasoned firewood and I recalled that before the renovations began we had moved a clay firepit to the edge of the yard. With a bit of scraping and brushing from a few available broken branches (that later became our kindling), we got a fire going in the little clay pit. Now we just needed a grill to cover the open mouth of our cooking contraption. We were in luck: though our charcoal grill was not functioning, the stainless-steel grill grate was just large enough to cover the entire mouth of the clay firepit. We were in business!

As we stoked the fire and watched a nice bed of coals take shape, we added three split and well-seasoned 16-inch slabs of wood and watched the fire rise. We seasoned the porterhouses with freshly cracked black peppercorns and sea salt. With our charcoal grill, we usually wait for white coals to accumulate at the bottom before we put the beef on the grate. But this combination—a shallow bed of coals and fresh raw flame from newly added timbers—immediately looked ready to do the job. Five minutes on each side was all it took.

Our contractor had recently given us a cutting block made from the reclaimed timbers of a 200-year-old barn. The two porterhouses, seared with lovely black marks, were a vision of beauty on the golden wood.

There is an art to grilling, a fine balance between the cut of meat, the temperature of flame, the quality of the smoke, and the right amount of time for these elements to work their magic. When that balance is just so—dinner becomes an event. Those porterhouses were just that. What might have been an utter disaster, thanks to a bit of ingenuity and a fair amount of luck, allowed us to dine like kings.

As great as those two steaks were, the best part was sharing the experience with my father. Food is a celebration of life—and who better to celebrate with than the ones you love?

NEW YORK STRIP

Makes 2 to 3 servings / Active Time: 15 minutes / Total Time: 1 hour and 30 minutes

This is the go-to steak for my family. Grilling the New York strip can be quick or long, depending on your grill's temperature. Letting the steaks rest at room temperature for an hour before grilling is not necessary, so if you are in a rush please feel free to skip it. However, if you do have the time, definitely let the steaks absorb the oil so that they are deliciously tender when pulled from the grill.

1   Remove the steaks from the refrigerator, rub them with the olive oil, and let rest at room temperature for 1 hour.

2   A half hour before cooking, bring your gas or charcoal grill to medium-high heat.

3   Once the grill is ready, about 425°F with the coals lightly covered with ash, season one side of the steaks with black pepper and sea salt.

4   Place the seasoned sides of the steaks on the grill. Wait 3 to 5 minutes until they are slightly charred. One minute before flipping, season the uncooked sides of the steaks with pepper and sea salt. Turn the steaks and grill for another 3 to 4 minutes for medium-rare and 4 to 5 minutes for medium. The steaks should feel slightly firm when poked in the center.

5   Remove the steaks from the grill and transfer to a large cutting board. Let stand for 10 minutes to allow the steaks to retain their juices. Serve warm and, if desired, garnish with rosemary.

NOTE: *For a more aromatic steak, light a fire using dry logs and burn down to coals. The grill will take about 45 minutes to preheat and the steaks will need to cook for about 1 minute longer on each side, but the results are worth the wait.*

INGREDIENTS

2 New York strip steaks, each about 1½ inches thick

2 tablespoons olive oil

Coarsely ground black pepper

Sea salt

Rosemary leaves, for garnish (optional)

RIB EYE

Makes 2 to 3 servings / Active Time: 15 minutes / Total Time: 1 hour and 30 minutes

A classic rib eye is my favorite cut of meat. When you go to your local butcher, look for organically raised and grass-fed beef, as the results will be worth the extra cost. The rib eye is best when well marbled and thick, so be sure to request this from your butcher. Consider serving this steak with some Shishito Peppers (see page 385) for some added kick.

1   Rub both sides of the steaks with olive oil and let rest at room temperature for about 1 hour.

2   A half hour before cooking, bring your gas or charcoal grill to medium-high heat.

3   Once the grill is ready, about 425°F with the coals lightly covered with ash, season one side of the steaks with the black pepper and sea salt. Place the seasoned sides of the steaks on the grill and cook for about 6 to 7 minutes until blood begins to pool on their tops. Season the tops of the steaks with pepper and salt while the base cooks. Once the steaks are charred, flip and cook for 4 to 5 more minutes for medium-rare and 5 to 6 more minutes for medium. The steaks should feel slightly firm when poked in the center. Remove the steaks from the grill and transfer to a large cutting board.

4   Let stand for 5 to 10 minutes, allowing the steaks to retain their juices. Serve warm.

NOTE: *I recommend cooking the rib eye to medium; medium-rare will be very chewy and tough. For a boneless rib eye, cook for 2 to 4 minutes less. Rib eye is often barbecued with rubs and marinades, though I tend to find it best when served with Cilantro Oil (see page 301).*

INGREDIENTS

2 bone-in rib eyes, each about 1¼ to 1½ inches thick

2 tablespoons olive oil

Coarsely ground black pepper

Sea salt

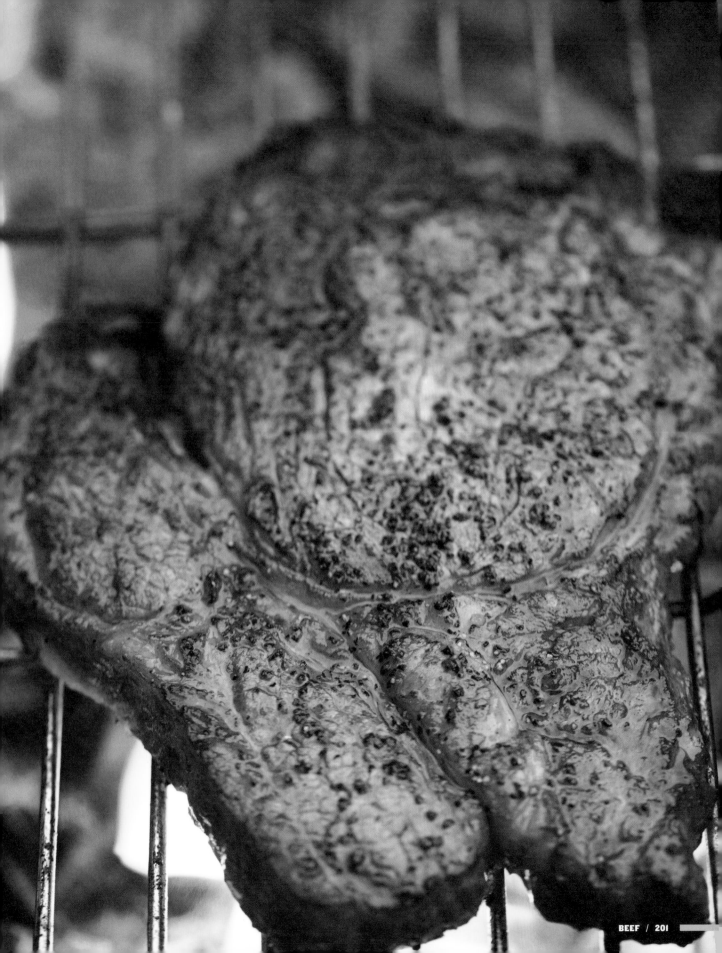

PORTERHOUSE

Makes 2 to 3 servings / Active Time: 20 minutes / Total Time: 1 hour and 45 minutes

This is by far one of the most filling steaks available, as it showcases both the New York strip and the filet mignon. Ask your butcher to keep a large part of the filet mignon intact for a true balance.

INGREDIENTS

2 porterhouse steaks, each about 1½ inches thick

4 tablespoons olive oil

Coarsely ground black pepper

Sea salt

Rosemary, for garnish (optional)

1   Rub both sides of the steaks with olive oil and let rest at room temperature for about 1 hour.

2   A half hour before cooking, bring your gas or charcoal grill to medium-high heat.

3   Once the grill is ready, about 425°F with the coals lightly covered with ash, season one side of the steaks with black pepper and sea salt. Place the seasoned sides of the steaks on the grill and cook for about 5 to 6 minutes, seasoning the tops of the steaks while the base cooks. Once the steaks are charred, flip and cook for 4 to 5 more minutes for medium-rare, and 6 to 7 for medium. The steaks should feel slightly firm when poked in the center.

4   Remove the steaks from the grill and transfer to a large cutting board. Let stand for 10 minutes, allowing the steaks to retain their juices. If desired, garnish with rosemary and serve warm.

TIP: *For some San Franciscan flare, combine the olive oil with a couple teaspoons of minced garlic before marinating the steaks.*

FILET MIGNON

Makes 2 to 3 servings / Active Time: 20 minutes / Total Time: 1 hour and 30 minutes

The filet is one of the harder steaks to grill due to its thickness and relatively small surface area. As such, I recommend using a seasoned cast-iron skillet over the grill for the initial searing and then transferring the filets to the oven.

1   Tie the butcher's twine tightly around each steak. Rub both sides of the steaks with 2 tablespoons of the olive oil and let rest at room temperature for about 1 hour.

2   A half hour before cooking, place the cast-iron skillet on the grate and bring your gas or charcoal grill to medium-high heat. Leave the grill covered while heating, as it will add a faint, smoky flavor to the skillet.

3   When the grill is ready, about 425°F with the coals lightly covered with ash, season one side of the steaks with the pepper and sea salt.

4   Spread the remaining olive oil in the skillet, and then place the steaks, seasoned sides down, into the skillet. Wait 2 to 3 minutes until they are slightly charred, seasoning the uncooked sides of the steaks with the pepper and salt while the base cooks. Turn the steaks and sear for another 2 to 3 minutes. Remove from the skillet and let rest uncovered for 30 minutes.

5   Preheat the oven to 400°F.

6   Put the steaks back into the cast-iron skillet and place in the oven. For medium-rare, cook for 11 to 13 minutes; for medium, cook for 14 to 15.

7   Remove the steaks from the oven, transfer to a large cutting board, and let stand for 10 minutes so the steaks retain their juices. Remove the butcher's twine from the steaks and serve warm.

TOOLS

1 to 2 feet butcher's twine

Cast-iron skillet

INGREDIENTS

2 filet mignon steaks, each about 2 to 2½ inches thick

3 tablespoons olive oil

Coarsely ground pepper

Sea salt

CHARRED FLANK STEAK

Makes 2 servings / Active Time: 15 minutes / Total Time: 1 hour and 25 minutes

The flank steak, often categorized as a chewy cut of meat, is one of the hardest to cook properly. Stay close to the grill after you put the steaks on, as it is very easy for them to be overcooked. Also, because the steak is very thin, be sure to prepare the grill to medium-high heat so that the edges are charred and crisp.

1 Rub the steak with a mixture of the olive oil, rosemary, and thyme. Let rest at room temperature for 1 hour.

2 A half hour before cooking, bring your gas or charcoal grill to medium-high heat.

3 Once the grill is ready, about 425°F with the coals lightly covered with ash, season one side of the steak with the black pepper and sea salt.

4 Place the seasoned side of the steak on the grill and cook for about 4 to 5 minutes, seasoning the uncooked side of the steak while the other side cooks. When the steak seems charred, gently flip and cook for 4 to 5 more minutes for medium-rare and 6 more minutes for medium. The steak should feel slightly firm when poked in the center.

5 Remove the steak from the grill and transfer to a large cutting board. Let stand for 6 to 8 minutes so that the steak can retain its juices. Slice the steak diagonally into long, thin slices. Serve warm.

NOTE: *Due to the flank steak's toughness, it is essential to slice it into very thin strips before serving.*

INGREDIENTS

1 flank steak, about 1 to 1½ pounds

2 tablespoons olive oil

Leaves from 2 sprigs of rosemary

Leaves from 2 sprigs of thyme

Coarsely ground black pepper

Sea salt

BALSAMIC-GLAZED FLANK STEAK WITH VIDALIA ONIONS & MUSHROOMS

Makes 2 to 3 servings / Active Time: 30 minutes / Total Time: 1 hour and 45 minutes

Flank steak's notorious toughness is tempered by the glaze, which adds a surprising tenderness.

1   Rub the steak with 2 tablespoons olive oil and let rest at room temperature for about 1 hour.

2   A half hour before cooking, bring your gas or charcoal grill to medium-high heat.

3   Prepare the Onions & Mushrooms. Heat the 2 tablespoons olive oil in a wide skillet over low heat. Add the onion slices and mushrooms and cook, while stirring frequently, for 15 to 20 minutes, until the onions are translucent and tender. Remove from heat and set aside.

4   Once the grill is ready, about 425°F and the coals are lightly covered with ash, season one side of the steak with the black pepper and sea salt. Place the seasoned side of the steak on the grill and cook for about 4 to 5 minutes, seasoning the uncooked side of the steak while the other side cooks. When the steak seems charred, gently flip and cook for 4 to 5 more minutes for medium-rare and 6 more minutes for medium. The steak should feel slightly firm when poked in the center.

5   Remove the steak from the grill and transfer to a large cutting board. Let stand for 6 to 8 minutes so that it can retain its juices.

6   Prepare the Balsamic Glaze. Add the balsamic vinegar to a small saucepan and bring to a boil over high heat. Reduce by half, about 6 to 7 minutes, and then stir in the clarified butter and rosemary. Remove from heat and season with black pepper and sea salt.

7   Slice the steak diagonally into long, very thin strips. Serve warm with the onions and mushrooms and drizzle the balsamic glaze on top.

TOOLS

Wide skillet

Saucepan

INGREDIENTS

FOR THE STEAK

1 flank steak, about 1 to 1½ pounds

2 tablespoons olive oil

Coarsely ground black pepper

Sea salt

FOR THE ONIONS & MUSHROOMS

2 tablespoons olive oil

1½ pounds Vidalia onions, sliced into ½-inch-thick pieces

1 pound mushrooms

FOR THE BALSAMIC GLAZE

1 cup balsamic vinegar

2 tablespoons butter, clarified

Leaves from 1 sprig of rosemary

Coarsely ground black pepper

Sea salt

BISTECCA ALLA FIORENTINA

Makes 2 servings / **Active Time: 30 minutes** / **Total Time: 1 hour and 45 minutes**

Cooked to medium-rare, these steaks will stand on their own. There is no real need for a side—maybe just a thin slice of lemon—but if you really want one, try the Tomatoes with Garlic (see page 393) for a dining experience that is out of this world.

INGREDIENTS

2 T-bone steaks, each about ¾ to 1¼ inches thick

4 garlic cloves, crushed

1 cup olive oil

Leaves from 1 sprig of rosemary

Coarsely ground black pepper

Sea salt

1 Place the steaks in a roasting pan or bowl, rub them with the garlic, ½ cup of the olive oil, and the rosemary, and let rest at room temperature for 1 hour.

2 A half hour before cooking, bring your gas or charcoal grill to medium-high heat.

3 Once the grill is ready, about 425°F with the coals lightly covered with ash, season one side of the steaks with the black pepper and sea salt. Place the seasoned sides of the steaks on the grill and cook for 5 minutes, basting the unseasoned sides with the remaining olive oil every 30 seconds. Season the top with salt and pepper, gently flip, and cook for 4 to 6 more minutes, basting until finished. The steak should feel slightly firm when poked in the center.

4 Remove the steaks from the grill and transfer to a large cutting board. Let stand for 6 to 8 minutes so that the steaks can retain their juices. Serve warm.

STEAK AU POIVRE

Makes 2 to 3 servings / Active Time: 25 minutes / Total Time: 1 hour and 30 minutes

This preparation often features a T-bone or porterhouse. However, because of the spice, it also works well with New York strip or filet mignon. If you decide to go with filet mignon, follow the recipe on page 204 for instructions on cooking the steak.

1   Rub both sides of the steaks with olive oil and let rest at room temperature for about 1 hour.

2   A half hour before cooking, bring your gas or charcoal grill to medium-high heat.

3   Seal the peppercorns in a small, sealable plastic bag and crush with the bottom of a cast-iron skillet.

4   Once the grill is ready, at about 425°F with the coals lightly covered with ash, press the crushed peppercorns and sea salt firmly into both sides of the steak. Place the steaks on the grill and cook for 4 to 5 minutes until they are slightly charred. Turn the steaks and grill for another 3 to 4 minutes for medium-rare, and 4 to 5 minutes for medium. The steaks should feel slightly firm when poked in the center.

5   Remove the steaks from the grill and transfer to a large cutting board. Let rest for 10 minutes, allowing the steaks to retain their juices.

6   Prepare the sauce. Heat the butter in a small saucepan over medium heat. Add the minced shallot and cook, while stirring occasionally, until it is softened, about 1 to 2 minutes.

7   Carefully add the Cognac and, if it flames, shake the pan and wait for the flame to burn out. Boil until the sauce has reduced by half.

8   Stir in the milk and cook until the sauce has slightly thickened, about 2 to 3 minutes. Add the parsley and sea salt.

9   Place the steaks onto warm plates and spoon the sauce on top.

TOOLS

Small saucepan

INGREDIENTS

FOR THE STEAKS

2 New York strip steaks, each about 1½ inches thick

2 tablespoons olive oil

6 tablespoons black peppercorns

Sea salt

FOR THE SAUCE

3 tablespoons butter, clarified

1 shallot, minced

½ cup Cognac

½ cup milk

2 tablespoons parsley, minced

Sea salt

PORTERHOUSE WITH CHIMICHURRI SAUCE

Makes 2 to 3 servings / Active Time: 35 minutes / Total Time: 2 hours

This Argentinian sauce goes well with any steak. It can be used as marinade, though this is a little risky because of the kick provided by the Fresno chili. If you're worried about the heat, try serving the sauce on the side.

1 Rub both sides of the steaks with olive oil and let rest at room temperature for about 1 hour.

2 A half hour before cooking, bring your gas or charcoal grill to medium-high heat.

3 Prepare the Chimichurri Sauce. Combine the vinegar, garlic, shallot, scallion, Fresno chili, lemon juice, and salt in a medium bowl and let rest for 15 minutes. Next, add the parsley, cilantro, and oregano, then gradually whisk in the olive oil. Set aside.

4 Once the grill is ready, at about 425°F with the coals lightly covered with ash, season one side of the steaks with the black pepper and sea salt. Brush a very light coating of the sauce along the bone.

5 Place the seasoned sides of the steaks on the grill and cook for about 5 to 6 minutes, seasoning the tops of the steaks while the other sides cook. Again, lightly coat the bone with the sauce. When the steaks are charred, flip and cook for 4 to 5 more minutes for medium-rare, and 6 to 7 for medium. The steaks should feel slightly firm when poked in the center.

6 Remove the steaks from the grill and transfer to a large cutting board. Let stand for 10 minutes, allowing the steaks to retain their juices. Serve warm with the Chimichurri Sauce on the side.

NOTE: *For those who would like even more heat in the sauce, substitute a habanero pepper for the Fresno chili.*

INGREDIENTS

FOR THE STEAKS

2 porterhouse steaks, each about 1½ inches thick

4 tablespoons olive oil

Coarsely ground black pepper

Sea salt

FOR THE CHIMICHURRI SAUCE

½ cup red wine vinegar

4 garlic cloves, minced

1 shallot, minced

½ scallion, minced

1 Fresno chili, minced

1 tablespoon fresh lemon juice

1 teaspoon sea salt

½ cup flat-leaf parsley, minced

½ cup cilantro, minced

2 tablespoons oregano, minced

¾ cup olive oil

CHIPOTLE RIB EYE

Makes 2 to 3 servings / Active Time: 20 minutes / Total Time: 1 hour and 30 minutes

This spicy steak is not for the faint of heart. Enjoy with a glass of red wine or a cold beer.

1 Prepare the rub. Place all of the ingredients in a small bowl and stir to combine. Set aside.

2 Rub a very thin layer of olive oil on both sides of the steaks and then generously apply the dry rub, firmly pressing it into the steak. Let rest at room temperature for at least 1 hour.

3 A half hour before cooking, bring your gas or charcoal grill to medium-high heat.

4 Once the grill is ready, at about 425°F with the coals lightly covered with ash, place the steaks on the grill and cook for about 6 to 7 minutes until blood begins to pool on the tops. When the steaks are charred, flip and cook for 4 to 5 more minutes for medium-rare, and 5 to 6 more minutes for medium. The steaks should feel slightly firm when poked in the center.

5 Remove the steaks from the grill and transfer to a large cutting board. Let stand for 5 to 10 minutes, allowing the steaks to retain their juices. Serve warm.

INGREDIENTS

FOR THE CHIPOTLE RUB

2 dried chipotle peppers, seeded and minced

1 tablespoon dried oregano

1 tablespoon dried cilantro

1 tablespoon coarsely ground black pepper

2 teaspoons ground cumin

1 teaspoon onion powder

½ teaspoon dry mustard

Sea salt

FOR THE STEAKS

1 tablespoon olive oil

2 rib eyes, each about 1¼ to 1½ inches thick

ANCHO CHILI-RUBBED LONDON BROIL

Makes 2 to 3 servings   /   Active Time: 30 minutes   /   Total Time: 1 hour and 30 minutes

The London broil is an economical steak that is perfect for large family gatherings. All you need to do is start with a tasty rub and finish by slicing the London broil into thin strips.

1   Prepare the rub. Combine the all of the ingredients in a small bowl and mix thoroughly. Set aside.

2   Rub a very thin layer of olive oil on both sides of the steak and then generously apply the dry rub, firmly pressing it into the steak. Let rest at room temperature for at least 1 hour.

3   A half hour before cooking, bring your gas or charcoal grill to medium-high heat.

4   Once the grill is ready, at about 425°F with the coals lightly covered with ash, place the steak on the grill. Cook until blood begins to pool on the top, about 4 to 5 minutes. When the steak is charred, flip and cook for another 3 to 4 minutes for medium-rare, and 5 to 6 for medium.

5   Remove the steak from the grill and transfer to a large cutting board. Let stand for 6 to 8 minutes to retain the juices. Slice the steak diagonally into long, thin slices and serve warm.

NOTE: *Due to the London broil's toughness, it needs to be sliced into very thin strips before serving.*

INGREDIENTS

FOR THE RUB

1 cup ancho chili powder

2 tablespoons paprika

1 tablespoon coarsely ground black pepper

1 tablespoon sea salt

2 teaspoons cumin

1 teaspoon cayenne pepper

1 teaspoon dry mustard

1 teaspoon oregano

FOR THE STEAK

1 to 2 tablespoons olive oil

1 London broil steak, about ¾ inch to 1 inch thick

BUTCHER'S STEAK

Makes 2 servings / Active Time: 15 minutes / Total Time: 5 hours and 30 minutes

The butcher's steak, or the hanger steak, is a phenomenal piece of meat when cooked properly. The marinade is key to this dish, as the oil provides the steak with a lovely amount of char.

1   Combine the ingredients for the marinade in a small, rectangular dish. Lay the steaks in the dish so that the marinade completely covers them. If not, add more olive oil until it does. Cover with aluminum foil, place in the refrigerator, and let rest for at least 4 hours.

2   Remove the steaks from the refrigerator and let stand at room temperature for about 1 hour.

3   A half hour before cooking, bring your gas or charcoal grill to medium-high heat.

4   Once the grill is ready, at about 425°F with the coals lightly covered with ash, remove the steaks from the marinade and season with the pepper and sea salt. Set the marinade aside.

5   Place the steaks on the grill. Cook for about 4 to 5 minutes, basting the steaks with the remaining marinade every 30 seconds. When the steaks are charred, gently flip and cook for 3 to 4 more minutes for medium-rare, and 5 minutes for medium. The steaks should feel slightly firm when poked in the center.

6   Remove the steaks from the grill and transfer to a large cutting board. Let stand for 5 to 10 minutes, allowing the steaks to retain their juices. Serve warm.

INGREDIENTS

FOR THE MARINADE

3 cups olive oil, plus more as needed

6 garlic cloves, crushed

3 sprigs of rosemary

3 sprigs of thyme

Juice from ¼ lemon

FOR THE STEAKS

2 butcher's steaks, each about 1 to 1½ pounds

Coarsely ground pepper

Sea salt

SKIRT STEAK WITH OLIVE TAPENADE

Makes 2 to 3 servings / Active Time: 30 minutes / Total Time: 1 hour and 50 minutes

The skirt steak is beloved for its distinct taste. However, because of how thin it is, it is very easy to overcook, causing it to become tough and chewy. As such, be sure to grill these steaks over direct heat and do not cook past medium.

1 Rub both sides of the steaks with olive oil and let rest at room temperature for about 1 hour.

2 Prepare the Olive Tapenade. Combine all of the ingredients in a medium bowl and mix thoroughly. Set aside.

3 A half hour before cooking, bring your gas or charcoal grill to extremely high heat.

4 Once the grill is ready, about 500°F to 600°F with the coals lightly covered with ash, season the steaks with the black pepper and sea salt. Place the steaks on the grill and spoon the tapenade onto the top of each steak. Cook for about 3 minutes and then flip. Again, add the tapenade and cook for about 2 to 3 minutes for medium-rare, and 3 to 4 for medium. The steaks should be very charred and slightly firm when poked in the center.

5 Remove the steaks from the grill and transfer to a large cutting board. Let stand for 5 to 10 minutes so that they retain their juices. Slice the steaks diagonally into long, thin slices and arrange the remaining tapenade on the side. Serve warm.

INGREDIENTS

FOR THE STEAKS

2 skirt steaks, each about 1 to 1½ pounds and ½ to ¾ inch thick

2 tablespoons olive oil

Coarsely ground black pepper

Sea salt

FOR THE OLIVE TAPENADE

1 cup Niçoise olives, pitted and chopped

½ cup olive oil

½ small shallot, minced

1 garlic clove, minced

Leaves from 1 sprig of rosemary, minced

1 anchovy fillet (optional)

1 tablespoon basil, minced

1 tablespoon flat-leaf parsley, minced

1 tablespoon capers, minced

1 tablespoon thyme

1 teaspoon red pepper flakes

RED WINE & HERB-MARINATED TRI-TIP STEAK

Makes 3 servings / Active Time: 45 minutes / Total Time: 14 hours

This steak is perfect for grilling out on the patio on the Fourth of July and enjoying just before the fireworks. Serve with Balsamic Peppers (see page 390).

1. The day before grilling, combine the ingredients for marinade in a large resealable plastic bag and let rest at room temperature. After 20 minutes, add the tri-tip roast to the bag so that it is completely submerged; more wine may be necessary. Seal, place in refrigerator, and let marinate overnight.

2. One hour before grilling, remove the bag from the refrigerator and let stand at room temperature.

3. Prepare your gas or charcoal grill, designating two sections: one for direct medium-high heat and the other for indirect heat.

4. Once the grill is ready, at about 425°F with the coals lightly covered with ash, remove the roast from the marinade and grill over direct heat for about 5 minutes per side. Next, move the roast to the indirect heat and cover the grill. Cook for another 20 to 30 minutes, flipping every 5 minutes. The tri-tip should be slightly firm and an instant-read thermometer should read around 125°F if inserted into the thickest section.

5. Remove the roast from the grill and transfer to a large cutting board. Let stand for 10 minutes, allowing the roast to retain its juices, and then slice across the grain into thin slices. Serve warm.

NOTE: *It is important that you marinate this steak overnight so that it becomes more tender when cooked on the grill.*

INGREDIENTS

FOR THE MARINADE

2 cups red wine, plus more as needed

2 tablespoons red wine vinegar

2 garlic cloves, crushed

Leaves from 2 sprigs of rosemary, minced

Leaves from 2 sprigs of thyme, minced

½ small white onion, minced

1 teaspoon fresh lemon juice

½ teaspoon dried oregano

Coarsely ground black pepper

Sea salt

FOR THE STEAK

1 tri-tip roast, about 1½ inches thick and 2 to 2½ pounds

FILET MIGNON WITH RED WINE REDUCTION

Makes 2 to 3 servings / Active Time: 30 minutes / Total Time: 2 hours

A red wine reduction is perfect company for the filet mignon. For a stunning sauce, prepare the reduction in the cast-iron skillet after it has been used for the filet.

1   Tie the butcher's twine tightly around each steak. Rub both sides of the steaks with 2 tablespoons of the olive oil and let rest at room temperature for about 1 hour.

2   A half hour before cooking, place the cast-iron skillet on the grate and bring your gas or charcoal grill to medium-high heat. Leave the grill covered while heating.

3   Once the grill is ready, at about 425°F with the coals lightly covered with ash, season one side of the steaks with the pepper and salt.

4   Spread the remaining olive oil in the skillet, and then place the steaks, seasoned sides down, into the skillet. Wait 2 to 3 minutes until they are slightly charred, seasoning the uncooked sides of the steaks with pepper and sea salt as they cook. Turn the steaks over and sear for another 2 to 3 minutes. Remove from the skillet and let rest, uncovered, for 30 minutes. Leave the skillet on the grill.

5   Preheat the oven to 400°F, and then prepare the reduction. Add the coconut oil to the skillet and wait 30 seconds, scraping the browned bits left by the filets from the bottom of the skillet. Stir in the shallot, garlic, and oregano and sauté for about 2 minutes, until tender and lightly browned.

6   Add the Port, dry white wine, and balsamic vinegar and simmer until reduced by half. Add the parsley and simmer for 1 minute. Remove the skillet from heat and pour the reduction into a small bowl. Season with pepper and salt, cover with aluminum foil, and set aside.

7   Place the filets back into the cast-iron skillet and transfer to the oven. For medium-rare, cook for 11 to 13 minutes, and for medium, cook for 14 to 15 minutes.

8   Remove the steaks from the oven and transfer to a large cutting board. Let stand for 10 minutes to retain their juices. Cut the twine, spoon the reduction over the filets, and serve warm.

TOOLS

1 to 2 feet of butcher's twine

Cast-iron skillet

INGREDIENTS

FOR THE STEAKS

2 filet mignon steaks, each about 2 to 2½ inches thick

3 tablespoons olive oil

Coarsely ground black pepper

Sea salt

FOR THE RED WINE REDUCTION

2 tablespoons coconut oil

½ shallot, minced

1 tablespoon garlic, minced

1 teaspoon fresh oregano, minced

1 cup Port wine

1 cup dry white wine

3 tablespoons balsamic vinegar

¼ cup fresh parsley, minced

Coarsely ground black pepper

Sea salt

NEW YORK STRIP WITH PIZZAIOLA SAUCE

Makes 2 to 3 servings / Active Time: 35 minutes / Total Time: 2 hours

This dish is destined to become one of your favorites. If you're looking for a vegetable to toss on the side, some grilled green beans are a lovely option.

1   Remove the steaks from the refrigerator and rub with 2 tablespoons of the olive oil. Let rest at room temperature for 1 hour.

2   A half hour before cooking, place the cast-iron skillet on the grate and bring your gas or charcoal grill to medium-high heat. Leave the grill covered while heating, as it will add a faint, smoky flavor to the skillet.

3   Once the grill is ready, at about 425°F with the coals lightly covered with ash, season one side of the steaks with the black pepper and sea salt.

4   Spread the remaining tablespoon of olive oil in the skillet, and then place the steaks, seasoned sides down, into the cast-iron skillet. Wait 2 to 3 minutes until they are slightly charred, seasoning the uncooked sides of the steaks with pepper and sea salt as they cook. Turn the steaks over and sear for another 2 to 3 minutes. Remove from the skillet and let rest, uncovered, for 30 minutes. Leave the skillet on the grill.

5   Preheat the oven to 400°F.

6   Prepare the sauce. Add the olive oil to the skillet, scraping the brown bits off the bottom of the pan. Once the oil is hot, add the garlic and cook until golden, about 30 seconds to 1 minute. Add the plum tomatoes, sun-dried tomatoes, oregano, rosemary, thyme, and red pepper flakes. Simmer for 15 minutes. Add the wine and basil and season with pepper and salt. Simmer for 20 more minutes, then remove the skillet from the grill and cover the pan with aluminum foil.

7   Transfer the steaks to a roasting pan and place them in the oven. Cook for 6 to 8 minutes for medium-rare, and 10 to 12 minutes for medium.

8   Remove the steaks, transfer to a large cutting board, and let stand for 10 minutes. Serve the steaks on warm beds of the sauce.

TOOLS

Cast-iron skillet

Roasting pan

INGREDIENTS

FOR THE STEAKS

2 New York strip steaks, each about 1½ inches thick

3 tablespoons olive oil

Coarsely ground black pepper

Sea salt

FOR THE PIZZAIOLA SAUCE

¼ cup olive oil

4 garlic cloves, finely chopped

2 pounds plum tomatoes, crushed by hand

¼ cup sun-dried tomatoes

1 sprig of oregano, minced

1 sprig of rosemary, minced

1 sprig of thyme, minced

1 teaspoon red pepper flakes (optional)

¼ cup dry white wine

½ cup basil, minced

Coarsely ground black pepper

Sea salt

TOOLS

6 to 8 cups hickory or
oak wood chips

Large, aluminum foil pan

Smoker box (for gas grill)

Saucepan

INGREDIENTS

FOR THE RUB

¼ cup paprika

3 tablespoons coarsely ground
black pepper

1 tablespoon chipotle
chili powder

1 tablespoon chili powder

2 teaspoons cayenne pepper

1 teaspoon ground cumin

1 teaspoon dried oregano

Sea salt

FOR THE BRISKET

1 center-cut beef brisket, 5 to 6
pounds and about ½ inch thick

2 tablespoons olive oil

FOR THE COLESLAW

¼ cup apple cider vinegar

¼ cup raw honey

1 garlic clove, minced

1 teaspoon celery salt

1 teaspoon coarsely ground black
pepper

1 teaspoon sea salt

½ teaspoon dry mustard

½ head of purple cabbage, shredded

½ head of green cabbage, shredded

2 carrots, peeled and minced

BLACKENED TEXAS BRISKET WITH COLESLAW

Makes 3 to 4 servings / Active Time: 8 to 9 hours / Total Time: 10 to 19 hours

Beef brisket is a cut from the chest muscles that is known for its toughness when cooked over high heat. To tenderize the meat, first grill the brisket at low heat, 225°F to 250°F, for a long period of time, about 5 to 7 hours. When cooked properly, the brisket will be tender and juicy. Coleslaw is the perfect accompaniment.

1. Prepare the rub. Place all of the ingredients in a small bowl and whisk thoroughly.

2. Rub the brisket with the olive oil and then generously apply the rub, kneading it into the meat. Wrap the brisket in plastic wrap and let rest at room temperature for 2 to 10 hours.

3. While waiting, soak the wood chips in water for 1 to 2 hours.

4. A half hour before cooking, bring your gas or charcoal grill to low heat, about 250°F. You want to designate two separate heat sections on the grill: one for direct heat and the other for indirect heat. To do this, simply arrange the coals toward one side of the grill or only turn on one of the burners.

5. Once the grill is ready and the coals are lightly covered with ash, drain 1 cup of the wood chips and spread over the coals or pour in a smoker box. Place the grate on the grill and then lay the brisket, fatty-side up, in the large aluminum pan. Position the pan over the cool section of the grill and then cover with the lid, aligning the air vent away from the wood chips so that the smoke billows around the brisket before escaping. Cook for 5½ to 6 hours, rekindling the fire with coals and fresh wood chips every hour or so. When the internal temperature reads 190°F to 200°F and the meat is very tender when pierced with a fork, remove from the grill. Transfer to a large cutting board and let stand for 20 to 30 minutes without touching.

6. Prepare the Coleslaw. Place a saucepan over medium-low heat and add all of the ingredients except for the cabbages and the carrots. Bring to a boil, reduce the heat, and simmer for 5 minutes. Place the cabbages and carrots in a medium-sized bowl. Remove the dressing from heat and slowly stir to combine with the cabbages and carrots. Refrigerate for 30 minutes.

7. Slice the brisket diagonally into ½-inch strips and serve with the Coleslaw.

HAMBURGERS WITH SUN-DRIED TOMATO PESTO AND PORTOBELLO MUSHROOMS

Makes 4 to 6 servings / Active Time: 1 hour and 15 minutes / Total Time: 2 hours and 15 minutes

These hamburgers take a little while to make—from the making of the pesto to the grilling of the Portobello Mushrooms. But they're so worth it!

1　Using your hands, combine the sirloin, chuck, and the shallot in a large bowl. Form the meat into patties about 1¼ to 1½ inches thick and season with the pepper and salt. To prevent the burgers from rising on the grill, take your thumb and make a small divot in the center of each patty. Let rest at room temperature for 1 hour.

2　Rub the mushrooms with 4 tablespoons of the oil and let rest at room temperature for 1 hour.

3　A half hour before cooking, bring your gas or charcoal grill to medium-high heat.

4　When the grill is 425°F, place the burgers and the mushrooms on the grill and cook for 3 to 4 minutes each side. Brush the mushrooms with the remaining olive oil once every minute. Transfer to a plate and let rest for 3 to 5 minutes.

5　Serve burgers on buns with lettuce, tomatoes, and red onion. Place a mushroom on top of each hamburger and top with a scoop of the pesto.

INGREDIENTS

FOR THE HAMBURGERS

1 pound ground sirloin

1 pound ground chuck

½ small shallot, minced

Coarsely ground black pepper

Sea salt

4 to 6 hamburger buns

1 head of romaine lettuce

2 tomatoes, sliced into ¼-inch pieces

1 red onion, sliced into ¼-inch pieces

Sun-Dried Tomato Pesto (see page 173)

FOR THE PORTOBELLO MUSHROOMS

4 to 6 large portobello mushrooms, stemmed

6 tablespoons olive oil

BEEF SHORT RIBS WITH RED WINE & BASIL MARINADE

Makes 4 to 6 servings / Active Time: 1 hour / Total Time: 8 hours

Beef short ribs are extremely soft and delicate after marinating. You can eat these with your hands, just remember to set out extra napkins.

1 Combine all of the ingredients for the marinade, except for the wine, in a large bowl or roasting pan. Add the short ribs and then pour in the wine. Transfer the bowl to the refrigerator and let rest for 4 to 6 hours.

2 Transfer the ribs from the marinade to a large cutting board or plate and let stand at room temperature for 1 hour. Season one side of the ribs with pepper and salt.

3 A half hour before cooking, bring your gas or charcoal grill to medium-high heat.

4 Once the grill is ready, at about 425°F with the coals lightly covered with ash, place the seasoned sides of the ribs on the grill and cook for about 4 minutes. Season the tops of the ribs while waiting. When the ribs are charred, flip them over and cook for 4 more minutes.

5 Transfer the ribs to a cutting board and let rest for 5 to 10 minutes. Serve warm.

INGREDIENTS

FOR THE MARINADE

2 cups basil leaves, minced

2 large carrots, minced

2 large onions, minced

2 garlic cloves, minced

1 scallion, minced

Leaves from 2 sprigs of thyme

Leaves from 2 sprigs of rosemary

Leaves from 2 sprigs of oregano

3 tablespoons olive oil

1 (750 ml) bottle of dry red wine

FOR THE SHORT RIBS

3 to 4 pounds beef short ribs, cut into 3- to 5-inch pieces

Coarsely ground black pepper

Sea salt

MEATBALLS IN MARINARA SAUCE

Makes 4 servings / Active Time: 1 hour / Total Time: 1 hour and 35 minutes

Think you're over homemade meatballs in a traditional marinara sauce? Throw them on the grill and rekindle that flame.

1 In a large bowl, use your hands to combine the beef, veal, and onion, and then slowly add in the almond flour. Let rest for 5 minutes and then add the rest of the ingredients, with the exception of the olive oil, and combine. Let stand at room temperature for 30 minutes.

2 A half hour before cooking, place a cast-iron skillet on your gas or charcoal grill and bring the grill to medium-high heat. Leave covered while heating, as it will add a faint, smoky flavor to the skillet.

3 Using your hands, form the meat mixture into firm balls that are 1½ to 2 inches wide. Place on a plate and set alongside the grill.

4 Once the grill is ready, at about 425°F and the coals lightly covered with ash, add the 2 tablespoons of olive oil to the skillet. When hot, add the meatballs one by one and sear on all sides for about 8 minutes, or until all sides are browned. Remove from the skillet and set aside.

5 Prepare the Marinara Sauce. Add the olive oil to the skillet, scraping off brown bits from the bottom. When the oil is hot, add the garlic and cook until golden but not browned, about 30 seconds to 1 minute.

6 Add the tomatoes, oregano, rosemary, thyme, and the seared meatballs. Simmer for 15 minutes. Add the wine, basil, pepper, and salt and simmer for 20 more minutes, until the meatballs are cooked through.

7 Remove the cast-iron skillet from the grill and spoon the meatballs and sauce into warm bowls.

NOTE: *For a spicier sauce, stir some Shishito Peppers (see page 385) in just before serving.*

TOOLS

Cast-iron skillet

INGREDIENTS

FOR THE MEATBALLS

1 pound ground beef

1 pound ground veal

1 large yellow onion, minced

¼ cup almond flour

3 garlic cloves, minced

2 large eggs, beaten

¼ cup flat-leaf parsley, minced

2 tablespoons basil leaves, minced

1 tablespoon red pepper flakes

Sea salt

2 tablespoons olive oil

FOR THE MARINARA SAUCE

¼ cup olive oil

4 garlic cloves, minced

2 pounds plum tomatoes, crushed by hand

Leaves from 1 sprig of oregano

Leaves from 1 sprig of rosemary

Leaves from 1 sprig of thyme

¼ cup dry white wine

½ cup basil, minced

1 teaspoon coarsely ground black pepper

Sea salt

TOOLS

Skewers

INGREDIENTS

FOR THE KEBABS

1 cup olive oil

¼ cup basil leaves

Leaves from 1 sprig of rosemary

1 garlic clove, minced

2 to 3 pounds top sirloin, cubed

FOR THE GRILLED CHERRY TOMATOES

3 tablespoons olive oil

8 to 12 cherry tomatoes

Leaves from 1 sprig of thyme

Coarsely ground black pepper

FOR THE SALSA VERDE

1 cup Italian parsley leaves

½ cup cilantro

¼ very small shallot

1 anchovy fillet

1 tablespoon capers

2 garlic cloves

1 teaspoon red wine vinegar

½ cup olive oil

MARINATED STEAK KEBABS WITH SALSA VERDE AND GRILLED CHERRY TOMATOES

Makes 3 to 4 servings / Active Time: 45 minutes / Total Time: 4 hours

Everyone loves a kebab. The Salsa Verde can be refrigerated overnight and served alongside anything, though it perfectly complements these kebabs.

1   Prepare the kebabs. Combine the olive oil, basil leaves, rosemary, and garlic in a large resealable bag, then add the cuts of meat. Seal the bag tight and let rest at room temperature for 2 to 3 hours.

2   A half hour before cooking, bring your gas or charcoal grill to medium-high heat.

3   When the sirloin has finished marinating, remove the pieces from the bag and place 3 to 4 pieces on each skewer.

4   Prepare the tomatoes. Drizzle the olive oil over the tomatoes in a bowl and sprinkle with the thyme. Season with black pepper and set aside.

5   Prepare the Salsa Verde. In a small food processor, add the parsley, cilantro, shallot, anchovy, capers, garlic, and red wine vinegar. Pulse into a thick paste. Remove from processor and place into a small bowl. Whisk in the olive oil and set aside.

6   Once the grill is ready, at about 425°F with the coals lightly covered with ash, place the kebabs on the grill. Grill the kebabs for about 8 to 9 minutes for medium-rare, 10 minutes for medium. Rotate the kebabs about every 2 minutes so the sirloin cooks evenly. After 4 minutes, add the tomatoes and cook until the skin is charred and blistered.

7   Remove kebabs and tomatoes from grill and transfer to a large cutting board. Let rest for 5 minutes and then serve warm with the Salsa Verde.

PRIME RIB ROAST

Makes 6 to 8 servings / **Active Time: 1 hour and 30 minutes** / **Total Time: 4 to 5 hours**

This recipe comes via my mother, who spends all of Christmas Day preparing this meal so that it is just right. This is a very simple dish to make, and as you prepare it more and more, you learn how to perfect it. Once you do that, break it out on a special occasion and serve with a bottle of your best red wine.

1 Rub the rib roast with olive oil and let rest at room temperature for 30 minutes.

2 Season the rib roast generously with salt and pepper and let rest for another 30 minutes.

3 Bring your gas or charcoal grill to medium-high heat.

4 Once the grill is ready, at about 425°F with the coals lightly covered with ash, place the rib roast in the middle of the grill and sear each side, including the ends, for about 2 to 3 minutes each.

5 Transfer the rib roast from the grill to a large cutting board and let sit for about 30 minutes.

6 Position a large roasting rack and pan in the middle of your oven and preheat to 350°F. You want the roasting rack to be very hot so that its grates will instantly sear the rib roast when you place it in.

7 On the cutting board, finely chop the leaves from 1 bunch of the thyme and rosemary and mix with salt and pepper. Roll the rib roast in the mixture so the entire roast is thinly coated. Mix the garlic cloves with the ½ teaspoon of olive oil so that it forms a paste. Rub the rib roast with the paste.

8 Divide the remaining 2 bunches of thyme and rosemary evenly and tuck into the creases between the ribs.

9 Place the rib roast fat side up onto the roasting pan and cook for 15 minutes per pound for rare, 20 minutes per pound for medium-rare.

10 Take the roast out of the oven when a meat thermometer reads 120°F. Transfer to a large cutting board and let stand for 10 to 15 minutes before carving. Serve with asparagus and cherry tomatoes for a festive-looking meal.

NOTE: *When cooking a rib roast, always remove from oven when the interior is about 5°F under the desired temperature. When you remove the rib roast and transfer to a cutting board, it will continue to cook for about 10 minutes, which will raise the internal temperature about 5°F.*

TOOLS

Large roasting rack and pan

INGREDIENTS

1 rib roast

½ teaspoon olive oil, plus more for rub

Sea salt

Coarsely ground black pepper

3 bunches of fresh thyme

3 bunches of fresh rosemary

Asparagus, for serving

Cherry tomatoes, for serving

LAMB

LAMB CHOPS

Makes 4 servings / Active Time: 15 minutes / Total Time: 1 hour and 30 minutes

This is a happy medium between the classic pork chop and New York strip. Lamb is a very tender meat, so use a light hand when you season with coarsely ground black pepper and sea salt.

1   Rub the lamb chops with the olive oil and let rest at room temperature for 1 hour.

2   A half hour before grilling, bring your gas or charcoal grill to medium-high heat.

3   Once the grill is ready, about 425°F with the coals lightly covered with ash, season one side of the chops with black pepper and sea salt.

4   Place the seasoned sides of the chops on the grill. Wait 3 minutes until they are slightly charred. One minute before flipping, season the uncooked sides of the chops with pepper and sea salt. Turn the chops and grill for another 3 minutes for medium-rare, and about 4 minutes for medium. The chops should feel slightly firm when poked in the center.

5   Remove the lamb chops from the grill and transfer to a large cutting board. Let stand for 10 minutes, allowing the lamb chops to retain their juices. Serve warm.

INGREDIENTS

4 lamb chops, each about 1¼ inches thick

2 tablespoons olive oil

Coarsely ground black pepper

Sea salt

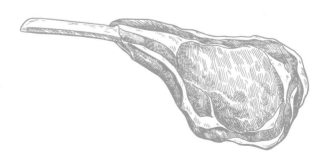

ROSEMARY AND LEMON LEG OF LAMB

Makes 4 servings / Active Time: 45 minutes / Total Time: 14 hours

Since the rosemary and lemon are relatively mellow, they go together perfectly when used in a marinade for a leg of lamb.

1 The day before you plan to grill, combine the olive oil, rosemary leaves, lemon juice, and garlic in a roasting pan and mix thoroughly.

2 Place the leg of lamb on a large cutting board. Season generously with coarsely ground black pepper and sea salt, kneading the lamb so that the pepper and salt are pressed in. Place the seasoned leg of lamb in the roasting pan.

3 Transfer the pan to the refrigerator and let the meat marinate overnight. Note that the marinade may not cover the meat entirely; in that case, flip the meat once halfway through the marinating process.

4 An hour before grilling, remove the leg of lamb from the refrigerator, transfer to a platter, and let stand at room temperature. Reserve the marinade.

5 A half hour before grilling, bring your gas or charcoal grill to medium-high heat.

6 When the coals are ready, at about 425°F with the coals lightly covered with ash, place the marinated leg of lamb on the grill and cook for about 16 minutes per side for medium-rare, 17 minutes for medium. While grilling, brush the reserved marinade on top of the lamb. When finished, transfer the lamb to a large cutting board and let rest for 15 minutes, allowing the meat to retain its juices.

7 Before serving, slice the lamb into ½-inch-thick diagonal strips. Serve warm.

INGREDIENTS

¾ cup olive oil

¼ cup rosemary leaves, coarsely chopped

Juice from 3 lemons

4 garlic cloves, minced

6-pound boneless leg of lamb, butterflied

Coarsely ground black pepper

Sea salt

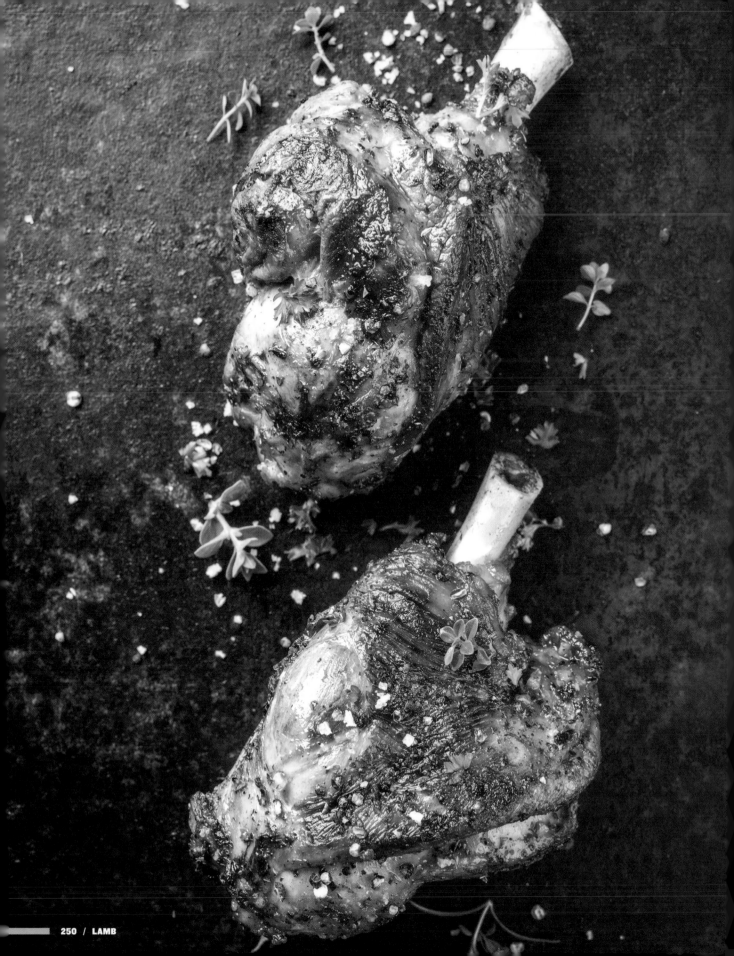

LEG OF LAMB WITH ROSEMARY-MUSTARD MARINADE

Makes 4 servings / Active Time: 30 minutes / Total Time: 1 hour

The rosemary and mustard work well when paired with a leg of lamb. In addition, the variation here encourages you to smoke the lamb, allowing for the richness of the mustard to become more pronounced.

1 In a small bowl, whisk together all of the ingredients other than the leg of lamb and lemon wedges.

2 Place the leg of lamb on a roasting rack. After setting a little aside, rub the marinade on the lamb, massaging it thoroughly into crevices of the meat. Cover the lamb with a sheet of aluminum foil and let stand at room temperature for about 2 hours.

3 A half hour before grilling, bring your gas or charcoal grill to medium-high heat.

4 When the coals are ready, at about 425°F with the coals lightly covered with ash, place the marinated leg of lamb on the grill and cook for about 16 minutes per side for medium-rare, 17 minutes for medium. While grilling, brush the reserved marinade on top of the lamb. When finished, transfer the lamb to a large cutting board and let rest for 15 minutes, allowing for the meat to retain its juices.

5 Before serving, slice the lamb into ½-inch-thick diagonal strips. Serve warm and garnish with wedges of lemon and additional parsley.

VARIATION

An hour before grilling, take 2 to 3 cups of hickory or oak wood chips and soak them in water. Just before you place the lamb on the grill, scatter the wood chips over the coals or place them in a smoker box. Cover the grill so that the smoke billows around the meat, and then cook for about 15 minutes for medium-rare.

INGREDIENTS

3 tablespoons olive oil

¼ cup rosemary leaves, minced

¼ cup Dijon mustard

4 garlic cloves, minced

1 large shallot, minced

Juice from ¼ small lemon

1 tablespoon flat-leaf parsley, minced, plus more for garnish

Coarsely ground black pepper

Sea salt

6-pound boneless leg of lamb, butterflied

Lemon wedges, for garnish

LAMB CHOPS WITH PARSLEY-MINT SAUCE

Makes 6 servings / Active Time: 30 minutes / Total Time: 1 hour and 30 minutes

Mint is one of the most common herb pairings for lamb, and the parsley and mint cooperate with each other. Don't hesitate to make a little more of the sauce, as it always seems to go quickly.

1 Place the lamb chops in a small bowl. In another small bowl, combine the garlic, rosemary, and olive oil. Pour the contents of the bowl over the lamb chops and then let rest at room temperature for 1 hour.

2 A half hour before grilling, bring your gas or charcoal grill to medium-high heat.

3 To make the sauce, combine the garlic, parsley, mint, anchovies (if desired), and lemon juice in a small bowl. Gradually whisk in the olive oil, and then season with black pepper and sea salt. Transfer to the refrigerator.

4 Once the grill is ready, at about 425°F with the coals lightly covered with ash, season one side of the chops with black pepper and sea salt. Place the seasoned sides of the chops on the grill. Wait 3 minutes until they are slightly charred. A minute before flipping, season the uncooked sides of the chops with pepper and salt. Turn the chops over and grill for another 3 minutes for medium-rare, and about 4 minutes for medium. The chops should feel slightly firm when poked in the center.

5 Remove the lamb chops from the grill and transfer to a large cutting board. Let stand for 10 minutes, allowing the lamb to retain its juices. Serve warm alongside the chilled Parsley-Mint Sauce.

INGREDIENTS

FOR THE LAMB CHOPS

6 lamb chops, each about 1¼ inches thick

3 garlic cloves, minced

3 tablespoons rosemary, minced

3 tablespoons olive oil

Coarsely ground black pepper

Sea salt

FOR THE PARSLEY-MINT SAUCE

1 garlic clove, minced

1 cup flat-leaf parsley, minced

¼ cup mint leaves, minced

2 anchovies, minced (optional)

Juice from ¼ lemon

½ cup olive oil

Coarsely ground black pepper

Sea salt

ROASTED RACK OF LAMB WITH GARLIC-HERB CRUST

Makes 5 to 6 servings / Active Time: 20 minutes / Total Time: 14 hours

Because a rack of lamb is very delicate, marinating overnight is essential to get that falling-off-the-bone texture you want.

1 Begin preparations for the lamb. The night before grilling, combine the olive oil, garlic, and lemon zest in a large resealable plastic bag. Pat the racks of lamb dry and season them with black pepper and sea salt, kneading the pepper and salt deeply into the meaty sections. Add the racks of lamb to the plastic bag and place it in the refrigerator. Let marinate overnight.

2 An hour and a half before grilling, remove the racks of lamb from the refrigerator and let rest uncovered at room temperature.

3 A half hour before grilling, bring your gas or charcoal grill to medium heat.

4 While the grill heats up, combine all of the ingredients for the crust in a small bowl. Next, take the racks of lamb and generously apply the mixture to it, making sure to apply the majority of the mixture on the meaty side of the racks.

5 Once the grill is ready, at about 400°F with the coals lightly covered with ash, place the meaty side of the racks of lamb on the grill and cook for about 3 to 4 minutes. When the crusts are browned, flip the racks of lamb over and grill for another 5 minutes for medium-rare.

6 Transfer the racks of lamb from the grill to a large cutting board and let rest for about 10 minutes before slicing between the ribs. Serve warm.

INGREDIENTS

FOR THE LAMB

2 tablespoons olive oil

2 garlic cloves, minced

1 teaspoon lemon zest

2 (8 rib) racks of lamb, about 1 pound each

Coarsely ground black pepper

Sea salt

FOR THE GARLIC-HERB CRUST

4 garlic cloves, minced

½ small shallot, minced

¼ cup flat-leaf parsley, chopped

2 tablespoons rosemary, minced

1 tablespoon thyme, minced

1 tablespoon olive oil

Coarsely ground black pepper

Sea salt

MARINATED LAMB KEBABS WITH MINT CHIMICHURRI

Makes 6 to 8 servings / Active Time: 30 minutes / Total Time: 5 to 14 hours

Kebabs are always a great route to take when cooking for a large gathering. This recipe easily serves 6 to 8 people, but can be cut in half to facilitate a smaller group. Just make sure not to halve the Mint Chimichurri: it's so good, you'll rarely have leftovers.

1 The night before you plan to grill, season the lamb cubes with coarsely ground black pepper and sea salt. Set aside.

2 In a large resealable plastic bag (if you need two, divide recipe between both bags), combine the remaining kebab ingredients except for the onions and peppers. Add the lamb cubes to the bag(s) and then transfer to the refrigerator, letting the meat marinate from 4 hours to overnight, the longer the better.

3 An hour and a half before grilling, remove the lamb from the refrigerator and let rest, uncovered and outside of the marinade, at room temperature.

4 Prepare the Mint Chimichurri. In a food processor, puree the garlic, parsley, mint, shallot, lime juice, and red wine vinegar. Slowly beat in the olive oil, and then remove the mixture from the processor. Season with black pepper and sea salt, cover, and set aside.

5 A half hour before grilling, bring your gas or charcoal grill to medium-high heat.

6 Pierce approximately 4 lamb cubes on each skewer, making sure to align the pieces of onion and pepper in between each cube.

7 Once the grill is ready, at about 425°F with the coals lightly covered with ash, place the skewers on the grill and cook for about 15 to 20 minutes. Transfer the kebabs to a large cutting board and let them rest for 5 minutes before serving with the Mint Chimichurri.

TOOLS

Skewers

Food processor

INGREDIENTS

FOR THE LAMB KEBABS

2 pounds lamb, cut into 1½-inch cubes

Coarsely ground black pepper

Sea salt

3 tablespoons olive oil

1½ cups red wine

4 garlic cloves, crushed

1 shallot, minced

2 teaspoons rosemary, minced

1 teaspoon ground cumin

2 red onions, roughly chopped

2 red bell peppers, roughly chopped

FOR THE MINT CHIMICHURRI

2 garlic cloves

2 cups flat-leaf parsley

2 cups mint leaves

1 small shallot

Juice from ¼ small lime

4 tablespoons red wine vinegar

½ cup olive oil

Coarsely ground black pepper

Sea salt

LAMB CHOPS WITH PAPRIKA-SALT RUB

Makes 4 servings / Active Time: 15 minutes / Total Time: 1 hour and 30 minutes

The paprika-and-salt combination is both soft and strong at the same time. If you are looking for a side, the mellowness of the Eggplant with Herbs (see page 401) pairs well with the slight bite of the rub.

1. An hour before grilling, brush the meat on the lamb chops with olive oil and let stand at room temperature.

2. In a small bowl, combine the remaining ingredients to make the rub. Using your hands, generously apply the rub to the lamb chops.

3. Bring your gas or charcoal grill to medium-high heat.

4. Once the grill is ready, at about 425°F with the coals lightly covered with ash, place the lamb chops on the grill and cook for about 4 minutes, or until the spices have browned. Turn the chops and cook for another 3 to 4 minutes for medium-rare, 4 to 5 minutes for medium.

5. Transfer the lamb rib chops to a large cutting board and let stand for 5 minutes before serving.

INGREDIENTS

12 lamb chops, each about 1 inch thick

2 tablespoons olive oil

2 tablespoons smoked paprika

1 tablespoon cumin seeds

2 teaspoons coriander seeds

½ teaspoon cayenne pepper

Coarsely ground black pepper

Sea salt

LAMB MEATBALLS IN SPICY TOMATO SAUCE

Makes 4 servings / Active Time: 45 minutes / Total Time: 2 hours and 30 minutes

The lamb meatball is very different than its beef-based counterpart. As they are heartier, they can be enjoyed for several days. These meatballs can be either an appetizer or a main course, but they work perfectly as a midday snack.

1 Prepare the Meatballs. In a large bowl, mix together the onion, garlic, eggs, cumin, oregano, and cinnamon. Next, knead the lamb into the bowl with your hands, making sure to toss the ingredients to thoroughly combine. Let rest for 5 minutes and then add in the parsley, pepper, and salt. Let stand at room temperature for 30 minutes.

2 A half hour before cooking, place a cast-iron skillet on your gas or charcoal grill and bring the grill to medium-high heat. Leave the cast-iron skillet on the grill while heating so that it develops a faint, smoky flavor.

3 Using your hands, form the lamb mixture into firm balls that are 1½ to 2 inches wide. Place on a platter and set alongside the grill.

4 Once the grill is ready, at about 425°F with the coals lightly covered with ash, add the 2 tablespoons of olive oil to the skillet. When hot, add the meatballs one by one and sear on all sides for about 8 minutes, or until all sides are browned. Remove from skillet and set aside.

5 Prepare the sauce. Add the olive oil to the skillet, scraping the brown bits from the bottom. Once the oil is hot, add the garlic and cook until golden but not browned, about 30 seconds to 1 minute. Add the tomatoes, oregano, rosemary, thyme, and the seared meatballs. Simmer for 15 minutes. Next, add the ground cumin, red pepper flakes, wine, basil, pepper, and salt and simmer for 20 minutes, or until the meatballs are cooked through.

6 Remove the cast-iron skillet from the grill and spoon the lamb meatballs and sauce into warm bowls.

TOOLS

Cast-iron skillet

INGREDIENTS

FOR THE MEATBALLS

1 white onion, minced

1 garlic clove, minced

2 whole eggs, beaten

1 teaspoon ground cumin

1 teaspoon dried oregano

½ teaspoon ground cinnamon

2 pounds ground lamb

¼ cup flat-leaf parsley, minced

Coarsely ground black pepper

Sea salt

2 tablespoons olive oil

FOR THE SPICY TOMATO SAUCE

¼ cup olive oil

3 garlic cloves, minced

1 (28 oz.) can of whole tomatoes

Leaves from 1 sprig of oregano

Leaves from 1 sprig of rosemary

Leaves from 1 sprig of thyme

½ teaspoon ground cumin

1 teaspoon red pepper flakes

¼ cup dry white wine

Handful of fresh basil leaves

Coarsely ground black pepper

Sea salt

PORK

PORK

WHEN IT COMES TO GRILLING over open flame or slow roasting at smoky, low temperatures, no other meat stands up to high and low heat better than pork. Whether you're cooking ribs or roasting a loin, pork offers some of the juiciest dishes that can be prepared on a grill. It is truly one of the most forgiving meats.

With more than 400 breeds around the world, farming pigs is big business, as pork is the most widely consumed meat globally. And with the rise of the farm-to-table movement, raising pigs has also become an artisan trade.

Large-scale pig farms may house as many as 5,000 pigs. Meanwhile, local, small-scale pig farms are focusing on raising and preserving heritage breeds, several of which have been nearly wiped out because they do not hold up well under the farming practices employed by large-scale enterprises. The good news is that discerning chefs are working hard at creating dishes that accentuate the subtle qualities of heritage pork. As consumers become more and more aware of the varieties in their pork choices, the demand for heritage pork is increasing.

Each breed has its own signature taste and purpose. The Tamworth is known for its delicious bacon, while the Duroc is known for being the most delectable and moist—perfect for roast loin of pork. If you're interested in finding heritage pork, seek the advice of local farmers and chefs. The flavor of freshly harvested pork ribs, loin, or chops is unmatched, and pork absorbs rubs, seasonings, and the aroma of hardwood smoke like no other.

Selecting the right cut of pork is essential when cooking over intense heat. This is especially true with pork chops, as the average chop is often far too thin for grilling. If you're looking for single-rib pork chops, you should never stray below a thickness of at least 1½ inches. For the ultimate pork chop experience, reach for the double-cut chop. I lean toward the rib chop, specifically center-cut and loin-cut chops. The center-cut is my preferred cut, as I like the balance of fat and meat. I may be in the minority, though. Many chefs and butchers prefer the loin-cut chop as it has a bit more fat, which helps keep the grilled meat juicy and flavorful. Whether you love a center-cut or a loin-cut chop, a double-cut chop gives you the wonderful flavor and tenderness that pork is famous for.

BASIC ROAST PORK LOIN

Makes 5 to 6 servings / Active Time: 1 hour and 15 minutes / Total Time: 2 hours

These basic ingredients bring out the pork's natural juices. Just be sure to use a pan that can go from the oven to the grill.

1   Preheat your grill and allow the coals to settle to a temperature of about 350°F. While the grill is heating, slowly sauté the olive oil and rosemary in a cast-iron skillet on your stove. While you can use a regular pan, be sure it is oven- and grill-safe, as you will be placing it directly on your grill.

2   Heat the rosemary and oil for about 10 to 12 minutes. Then, rub the pork loin with black pepper and sea salt and place the pork loin into the pan, turning it so the entire loin is covered with the heated oil.

3   Baste for 5 to 10 minutes until the loin begins to brown. Once your grill has reached the desired temperature, move the skillet to your grill.

4   Cover your grill and allow the pork to cook for 45 minutes, turning and basting the pork occasionally so all sides are thoroughly browned.

5   After about 45 minutes, remove the pork loin from the skillet and place directly on the grate. Continue to baste your pork loin using the infused oil from the pan, turning the loin so the entire roast is evenly cooked. Baste and turn for an additional 15 minutes, or until the roast meets your desired temperature.

6   Remove from heat and let the loin rest for 10 to 12 minutes. Carve and serve with sides of your choice.

TOOLS
Cast-iron skillet

INGREDIENTS
5 tablespoons olive oil

2 sprigs of rosemary

2¼-pound pork loin

Coarsely ground black pepper

Sea salt

PINEAPPLE PORK LOIN

Makes 5 to 6 servings / Active Time: 1 hour and 30 minutes / Total Time: 2 hours and 15 minutes

This classic is tailor-made for company. The acidity of the pineapple is complemented by the sweetness of the honey, making this a mouthwatering meal worthy of any occasion.

1 Preheat your gas or charcoal grill to medium-low heat.

2 While the grill is heating, slowly sauté the olive oil and rosemary in a cast-iron skillet on your stove.

3 After the oil and rosemary have been thoroughly heated and the oil is infused with the flavors of the sprigs, add half of the pineapple, the honey, water, and ginger. Stir and bring the mixture to a gentle boil.

4 Rub the pork loin with pepper and salt and then place the pork loin into the pan, turning it so the entire loin is covered with the basting sauce for 5 to 10 minutes at medium heat until the loin begins to brown. Once your grill has reached 350°F, move the skillet to your grill.

5 Cover the grill and allow the pork to cook for 45 minutes, turning and basting the pork occasionally so all sides are browned.

6 After about 45 minutes, remove the pork loin from the pan and place it directly on the grate. Baste with the remaining pineapple to create a golden-brown glaze as you turn the loin for another 15 minutes.

7 Remove from heat and let the loin rest for 10 to 12 minutes. Carve and serve with sides of your choice.

TOOLS

Cast-iron skillet

INGREDIENTS

5 tablespoons olive oil

2 sprigs of rosemary

1 cup pineapple, crushed

¼ cup honey

¼ cup water

1 teaspoon ginger, grated

2¼-pound pork loin

Coarsely ground black pepper

Sea salt

ROAST PORK WITH ORANGE SAUCE

Makes 5 to 6 servings / Active Time: 1 hour and 30 minutes / Total Time: 2 hours and 30 minutes

Orange, garlic, chili powder, and oregano come together beautifully in this grilled roast pork that is anything but bland.

1 Preheat your gas or charcoal grill to medium-low heat. Place a cast-iron skillet on the grill while it heats up.

2 When the grill is 350°F, heat the olive oil in the cast-iron skillet and spread to cover the entire bottom of the pan. Once the oil begins to glisten, gently pour in the fresh orange juice. Add the orange zest, garlic, bay leaves, chili powder, and oregano and stir until the ingredients are well combined and heated through.

3 Rub the pork loin with pepper and salt and then place it in the skillet.

4 Cover the grill and allow the pork to cook for about 1 hour and 15 minutes, basting every 15 to 20 minutes or so.

5 After roasting for 1 hour and 15 minutes, remove the loin from the pan and place directly on the grill. Continue basting and turning the pork so that it cooks evenly.

6 When the roast is browned and seared, remove it from the grill and allow it to sit for 10 minutes before carving.

TOOLS
Cast-iron skillet

INGREDIENTS
3 tablespoons olive oil

1½ cups fresh orange juice without pulp

1 to 2 teaspoons orange zest

1 garlic clove, chopped

2 bay leaves

Pinch of chili powder

Pinch of dried oregano

2½-pound pork loin

Coarsely ground black pepper

Sea salt

BRAISED PORK WITH ROSEMARY

Makes 5 to 6 servings / Active Time: 45 minutes / Total Time: 1 hour and 45 minutes

The rosemary leaves catch on fire and burn while roasting, lending a charred sweetness to the pork.

1 Preheat your gas or charcoal grill to medium-low heat. Place a cast-iron skillet on the grill as it heats up.

2 Push the rosemary into the pork loin. This will help infuse the rosemary throughout the pork and keep it from falling off during the cooking process. Leave a little bit of each leaf sticking out to catch the flames, as this will add to the overall taste. Brush and coat the pork loin with 2 tablespoons of the olive oil.

3 When the grill is 350°F, place the roast in the skillet with the remaining oil. Cook the pork, while turning, until it has a lovely golden brown color.

4 Add the remaining ingredients to the skillet and cook for about an hour. If you can control the temperature of your grill, lower the heat so everything gently simmers for 1½ hours.

5 Just before the pork appears to be done, remove it from the pan and place it directly on the grill to sear.

6 When the exterior is charred, remove the pork from the grill and let it stand for 10 to 12 minutes. Slice thin before serving, season with salt and pepper, and use some of the cooked juices as a light gravy.

VARIATION

For a lighter seasoning, substitute 3 tablespoons freshly chopped dill for the rosemary.

TOOLS

Cast-iron skillet

INGREDIENTS

Leaves from 2 sprigs of rosemary

2¼-pound boneless pork loin

8 tablespoons olive oil

1 garlic clove, crushed

½ onion, chopped

¾ cup white wine

1 tablespoon white vinegar

Sea salt

Coarsely ground black pepper

CLASSIC DOUBLE-CUT RIB CHOPS

Makes 4 to 6 servings / Active Time: 25 minutes / Total Time: 45 minutes

Pork's capacity to provide wonderful flavor with nothing more than a bit of seasoning and the heat of a grill is on display in this simple dish.

1 Preheat your grill to 400°F. Designate two separate heat sections on the grill, one for indirect heat and the other for direct heat. To do this, simply arrange the coals toward one side of a charcoal grill, or leave one of the burners off on a gas grill.

2 Place the chops over direct heat and sear both sides of the chops until browned, about 5 minutes per side. Keep a eye on the grill, as fat drippings can create flare-ups that will char the meat.

3 Once the chops are seared, move them over indirect heat and let them cook until an instant-read thermometer reads 135°F for medium-rare and approximately 145°F for medium. Season with salt and pepper before serving.

NOTE: *If you want more flavor from your pork, try adding different hardwoods to your fire (or in your smoker box if cooking over a gas grill). Apple and cherry are good choices, adding a mild but lovely fruitiness to pork and poultry dishes.*

INGREDIENTS

4 to 6 double-cut rib chops

Sea salt

Coarsely ground black pepper

KILLER BBQ SPARE RIBS

Makes 6 to 8 servings / Active Time: 1 hour and 45 minutes / Total Time: 4 to 5 hours

Slow roasting the ribs in the oven at a low temperature for about 3 hours allows the acids and seasonings to gently tenderize the meat. The low heat loosens the meat from the bone so it can be pulled away without any fuss. Using a covered roasting pan keeps the moisture inside, which helps the seasoning seep into the meat.

TOOLS

Large saucepan

Roasting pan with cover

INGREDIENTS

3 garlic cloves, 2 sliced very thin; 1 minced

1 cup honey

⅓ cup dark molasses

⅓ cup dark maple syrup

1½ tablespoons paprika

1 teaspoon sea salt

1½ teaspoons coarsely ground black pepper

1 tablespoon ancho chili powder

2 teaspoons ground cumin

½ cup apple cider vinegar

1½ cups tomatoes

5 to 6 oz. tomato paste

¼ cup hot sauce

¼ cup Worcestershire sauce

1½ tablespoons fresh lemon juice

5 tablespoons onions, chopped

1 teaspoon mustard powder

½ pineapple, cubed

4 to 5 pounds spare ribs

1   Preheat the oven to 325°F. Meanwhile, combine all of the ingredients except the ribs in a large saucepan. Cook over medium-low heat until it thickens. Line the bottom of the roasting pan with a thick layer of the sauce.

2   Place the racks of ribs in the roasting pan and coat them each with the sauce. Cover the pan, place it in the oven, and cook for 2½ to 3 hours.

3   About 15 to 20 minutes before the ribs have finished cooking in your oven, bring your grill to medium heat.

4   When the grill is 400°F, remove the ribs from the oven and place them directly on the grill. While cooking, baste your ribs with the sauce in the roasting pan. Once blackened, remove the ribs from the grill and place them on a serving tray. Allow the ribs to cool before serving.

PORK PORCHETTA

Makes 4 to 6 servings / Active Time: 1 hour and 30 minutes / Total Time: 14 hours

This recipe has plenty of flavor, but if you're looking to take it in a slightly different direction add some soaked apple wood chips to your fire.

1 Allow the pork to come to room temperature and season it with salt and pepper.

2 In a large saucepan, warm the olive oil and the oil from the tin of anchovies over high heat. Add the garlic and onion and cook until they are near brown. Stir in the rosemary, red pepper flakes, fennel seeds, orange and lemon zest, and 3 or 4 anchovies. Use a wood spatula to break up the anchovy fillets while stirring. About 1 minute before you remove the saucepan from heat, add the orange juice and stir. Remove the pan from heat and allow to cool to room temperature.

3 Cover the bottom of a casserole dish with the marinade and place the pork shoulder in it. Use the remaining marinade to completely coat the pork shoulder, making sure to work it into the meat. Cover the dish and refrigerate overnight.

4 Remove the marinated pork from the refrigerator several hours before you plan to cook and allow to come to room temperature. Preheat your gas or charcoal grill to between 300°F and 400°F.

5 Place the pork shoulder directly on the preheated grill. Do not use the marinade in the dish to baste the pork, as it has been in contact with raw meat.

6 Cover the grill and cook the shoulder until the desired internal temperature is reached. Remove the pork and allow it to cool for 10 to 15 minutes before slicing thin. Serve warm.

TOOLS

Large saucepan

INGREDIENTS

2½- to 3-pound boneless pork shoulder, butterflied

½ cup sea salt

½ cup freshly ground black pepper

2 to 3 tablespoons olive oil

1 small tin of anchovies packed in olive oil

4 garlic cloves, sliced very thin

1 onion, chopped

Leaves from 1 or 2 sprigs of rosemary

2½ tablespoons red pepper flakes

1½ tablespoons fennel seeds

Zest and juice of 1 orange

Zest of 1 lemon

SLOW PORK CARNITAS TACOS WITH SPICY TOMATILLO SALSA

Makes 6 servings / Active Time: 1 hour / Total Time: 4 hours and 30 minutes

Combining the juiciness of pork with the heat of the Spicy Tomatillo Salsa puts a new spin on this classic meal.

1 Preheat your gas or charcoal grill to medium-low heat.

2 Trim the pork shoulder of excess fat and discard. Next, cut the pork shoulder into 3- to 4-inch cubes and place them in a large bowl. Add the lime juice, sea salt, cumin, chili powder, all-purpose seasoning, oregano, garlic powder, onion powder, and black pepper to the bowl and stir until the pork is evenly coated. Transfer the cubes of pork shoulder to a large Dutch oven covered with a lid, and place alongside the grill.

3 Once the grill is ready, at about 325°F with the coals lightly covered with ash, place the covered Dutch oven on the grill and cover the grill. Cook the pork for about 3 to 4 hours, making sure to keep the grill's temperature between 300°F and 325°F.

4 Prepare the salsa. Place the tomatillos in a saucepan and cover with water. Place over medium-high heat on the stovetop, bring to a boil, and cook for 10 minutes. After 10 minutes, remove the tomatillos from the saucepan and place in a food processor along with the remaining ingredients. Pulse until smooth.

5 After 3 hours, open the Dutch oven and check the pork. If finished, the pork should fall apart when touched by a fork. If not done, continue to cook and check the pork every 10 to 15 minutes to prevent overcooking.

6 Remove the Dutch oven from the grill and use two forks to shred the pork shoulder.

7 Serve warm with corn tortillas, cilantro, jalapeño, and onion.

TOOLS

Dutch oven

Saucepan

INGREDIENTS

FOR THE PORK CARNITAS

3-pound pork shoulder

1 tablespoon lime juice

2 teaspoons coarse sea salt

2 teaspoons ground cumin

1 teaspoon chili powder

2 teaspoons all-purpose seasoning

1 teaspoon Mexican oregano

1 teaspoon garlic powder

1 teaspoon onion powder

1 teaspoon coarsely ground
black pepper

15 to 20 corn tortillas, homemade
(see pages 402–3) or store-bought

1 bunch of cilantro, chopped,
for serving

2 jalapeño peppers, chopped,
for serving

1 onion, chopped, for serving

FOR THE SPICY TOMATILLO SALSA

10 tomatillos, husked and rinsed

1 small onion, chopped

2 garlic cloves, minced

¼ cup fresh cilantro, chopped

1 jalapeño pepper, chopped

Coarsely ground black pepper

Sea salt

CHORIZO TACOS WITH AL PASTOR SALSA

Makes 6 servings / Active Time: 30 minutes / Total Time: 1 hour

This is one of the easiest grilled taco recipes. The most important element is buying quality chorizo. The better the chorizo, the better the taco.

1 Preheat your gas or charcoal grill to medium-low heat, leaving a cast-iron skillet on the grate while the grill warms.

2 Prepare the Al Pastor Salsa. Place all ingredients in a small bowl and stir to combine. Place in refrigerator and let chill.

3 Once the grill is ready, at about 350°F with the coals lightly covered with ash, heat the olive oil in the skillet for about 30 seconds. Next, add the chorizo to the frying pan and cook, while stirring frequently, for about 8 to 10 minutes, until the chorizo is browned and crisp.

4 Once crisp, remove the chorizo from the pan and set on a bed of paper towels so that the oils drain from the meat. Let rest for 5 minutes, and then add to tortillas. Top with Al Pastor Salsa, and garnish with cilantro, onion, and jalapeño.

VARIATION

Consider adding crisp potatoes to your chorizo tacos. Peel 2 russet potatoes and cook for 15 minutes in a pot of boiling water. They should be easily pierced with a fork once done. Remove and let cool. Next, while cooking the chorizo, add the potatoes to the pan and chop them up using a fork so the chorizo and potatoes are thoroughly combined.

TOOLS

Cast-iron skillet

INGREDIENTS

FOR THE AL PASTOR SALSA

1 cup pineapple, cut into ¼-inch cubes

¼ cup cilantro, chopped

3 tablespoons red onion, chopped

Juice from 1 lime

Sea salt

FOR THE CHORIZO TACOS

1 tablespoon extra virgin olive oil

1½ pounds chorizo, casing removed and chopped

10 to 15 corn tortillas, homemade (see pages 402–3) or store-bought

1 bunch of cilantro, minced, for garnish

1 white onion, minced, for garnish

1 jalapeño pepper, minced, for garnish

POULTRY

POULTRY

POULTRY IS A CLOSE SECOND TO PORK in its popularity worldwide, and it offers the most extreme range of any meat. Chicken, the most fundamental meat within the poultry family, is mild compared to duck and quail, which are much oilier with a higher fat content, much like the dark meat of chicken legs. Turkey lies somewhere in between, boasting both hearty white meat and dense thighs and legs. It is extremely important to understand the qualities of each bird within the poultry family before setting out to prepare them.

A dish that still resonates with me was a skin-on chicken breast prepared by chef Derek Bissonnette at the renowned White Barn Inn in Kennebunk, Maine. Derek's classic, delicate approach to preparing the chicken kept the meat moist and succulent even after it had been roasted over high heat. The strong flavors in the grill-charred skin balanced elegantly against those of the tender meat. As I learned from Derek, when it comes to grilling any type of poultry, it is essential to marinate, baste, or butterfly the bird so that it does not overcook and become tough.

All in all, poultry is a very versatile meat, although it can take a little while to grow comfortable with grilling it. The recipes found in this chapter present chicken in a number different of ways—from milder preparations like Lemon and Garlic Chicken (see page 309) to barbecue favorites such as Smoked and Pulled BBQ Chicken Sandwiches (see pages 298–99). I've also picked a variety of recipes for spice lovers—with dishes inspired by Mexican, Indian, and Asian cuisines. The Jamaican Jerk Chicken with Grilled Pineapple (see pages 292–93) is one of my personal favorites. And to really impress your guests with your grilling skills, try the Chicken Under a Brick with Cilantro Oil (see page 301).

From chicken, we turn to a couple of unusual turkey recipes, such as the Brined Turkey my family and I enjoy on Thanksgiving (see page 313). The brining of the turkey helps lock in the moisture while cooking. The Cajun Turkey with Cranberry Sauce (see page 314) is the perfect meal if you're looking to take your leftovers up a notch. Finally, there are game-oriented recipes such as the Cider-Glazed Cornish Hens (see page 317) and Quail with Citrus Spinach Salad (see page 318).

TOOLS

Aluminum pan

INGREDIENTS

FOR THE CHICKEN

½ cup plus 1 tablespoon olive oil

½ small white onion, minced

¼ cup flat-leaf parsley, minced

Leaves from 2 sprigs of rosemary, minced

2 garlic cloves, crushed

2 tablespoons red wine vinegar

4- to 5-pound chicken

Coarsely ground black pepper

Sea salt

FOR THE CHIPOTLE CAULIFLOWER

2 large heads of cauliflower, cut into florets

¼ cup olive oil

Juice from ½ lime

3 garlic cloves, diced

1 tablespoon chipotle powder

2 teaspoons paprika

2 tablespoons basil leaves, sliced

Coarsely ground black pepper

Sea salt

RED WINE-MARINATED CHICKEN WITH CHIPOTLE CAULIFLOWER

Makes 4 to 6 servings / Active Time: 1 hour and 30 minutes / Total Time: 9 hours

For the marinade, be sure to let the bird soak as long as you can. If you really want to bring out the spiciness of the Chipotle Cauliflower, throw some soaked wood chips over the fire.

1   In a large bowl, combine the ½ cup of olive oil, onion, parsley, rosemary, garlic, and vinegar. Place the chicken breast side down into the marinade, keeping in mind that the chicken will not be fully submerged. Let soak for 4 to 6 hours, turning the chicken over when 1 hour of marinating time remains.

2   Remove the chicken from the marinade and season with pepper and sea salt. Let the chicken stand at room temperature for 30 minutes to 1 hour. A half hour before grilling, bring your gas or charcoal grill to medium heat.

3   While waiting, prepare the cauliflower. Combine the cauliflower florets, olive oil, and lime juice in a medium bowl. Stir in the remaining ingredients. Transfer into an aluminum pan and set aside.

4   Once the grill is ready, at about 400°F with the coals lightly covered with ash, place the chicken on the grill, breast side up. Cover the grill and cook for about 40 minutes. Before flipping, brush the top of the chicken with the remaining tablespoon of olive oil. Turn and cook for about 15 more minutes, until the skin is crisp and a meat thermometer inserted into the thickest part of the thigh reads 165°F.

5   Remove the chicken, transfer to a large cutting board, and let stand for 15 minutes.

6   Position the aluminum pan of cauliflower on the grill and cover with a lid. Cook for 8 to 9 minutes until the florets are crisp. Remove from grill and serve alongside the chicken.

CHICKEN WITH ARUGULA AND BALSAMIC-ROSEMARY VINAIGRETTE

Makes 4 servings / Active Time: 25 minutes / Total Time: 2 hours and 30 minutes

A simple dinner, but certain to delight. Be sure to keep the grill covered while cooking to let the skin crisp properly.

1 Combine the chicken thighs, lemon juice, Dijon mustard, leaves from the 2 rosemary sprigs, garlic, and 4 tablespoons of olive oil in a large resealable plastic bag. Seal and thoroughly combine with your hands. Let rest at room temperature for 2 hours.

2 A half hour before grilling, bring your gas or charcoal grill to medium-high heat.

3 Add the remaining sprig of rosemary and the remaining olive oil to a small saucepan and set over medium-high heat. Bring to a simmer and then remove from heat. Discard the sprig of rosemary and pour the oil into a small bowl. Set aside.

4 When the grill is ready, at about 425°F with the coals lightly covered with ash, remove the chicken from the marinade and season with black pepper and sea salt. Then, place the chicken thighs skin side down on the grill and let cook for about 9 minutes. Flip and cook for 4 to 5 more minutes. Once finished, the chicken thighs should feel springy when poked.

5 Remove the chicken thighs from grill and place on a large cutting board. Let rest for 5 to 10 minutes.

6 While waiting, stir the balsamic vinegar and red pepper flakes into the rosemary oil. Season with black pepper and sea salt. Drizzle this mixture over the arugula and divide between the plates. Position chicken thighs on top of the arugula and serve with lemon wedges.

TOOLS

Saucepan

INGREDIENTS

8 bone-in, skin-on chicken thighs

Juice from ½ lemon

2 tablespoons Dijon mustard

3 sprigs of rosemary, leaves removed from 2

1 garlic glove, minced

½ cup plus 4 tablespoons olive oil

Coarsely ground black pepper

Sea salt

2 tablespoons balsamic vinegar

¼ teaspoon red pepper flakes

4 cups arugula, stemmed

½ lemon, sliced into wedges, for serving

TOOLS

Food processor

2 to 3 cups hickory or oak wood chips

Smoker box (for gas grill)

INGREDIENTS

1 large yellow onion, halved

4 to 5 habanero peppers, stemmed and seeded

3 scallions

2-inch piece of ginger, peeled and chopped

8 garlic cloves

1 teaspoon ground cinnamon

1 teaspoon ground nutmeg

2 teaspoons allspice

1 teaspoon dried thyme

1 teaspoon cayenne pepper

¼ teaspoon ground cloves

2 teaspoons coarsely ground black pepper, plus more to taste

2 teaspoons sea salt, plus more to taste

Juice from ½ small lime

½ cup olive oil

1½ cups warm water (100°F)

4 bone-in, skin-on chicken thighs

4 skin-on chicken legs

1 pineapple, peeled, cored, and cut into strips

JAMAICAN JERK CHICKEN WITH GRILLED PINEAPPLE

Makes 4 servings / Active Time: 45 minutes / Total Time: 1 to 2 days

The jerk spice on the chicken is not for the faint of heart. The chicken is just as good cold on a sandwich the next day, so long as you use high-quality rolls.

1. Place all of the ingredients except for the chicken and the pineapple in a food processor and puree until combined. Remove the marinade and place into a large resealable plastic bag. Add the chicken thighs and legs, making sure they are fully submerged in the marinade. Refrigerate for 24 to 48 hours.

2. Soak the wood chips in water for 1 to 2 hours.

3. Remove the bag from the refrigerator 1 hour before grilling. Transfer the chicken thighs and legs from the marinade to a plate and let rest, uncovered, at room temperature.

4. A half hour before grilling, bring your gas or charcoal grill to medium heat. Designate two separate heat sections on the grill, one for indirect heat and the other for direct heat. To do this, simply arrange the coals toward one side of your charcoal grill or turn off one of the burners on your gas grill.

5. Season the pineapple lightly with black pepper and sea salt.

6. Once the grill is ready, at about 400°F with the coals lightly covered with ash, remove the wood chips from the water and scatter them over the coals or place them in a smoker box. Place the pineapple over indirect heat and cook for about 3 to 4 minutes on each side. Remove from the grill once golden and set aside.

7. Place the chicken thighs and legs skin side down on the grill over direct heat. Cover the grill and cook for 6 to 7 minutes. Flip the chicken over and place over indirect heat. Cover and cook for 4 to 5 more minutes. When finished, the chicken should feel springy when poked.

8. Remove the chicken from the grill and transfer to a large cutting board. Let rest for about 5 minutes and then serve with the pineapple.

GINGER-SESAME CHICKEN

Makes 4 servings / Active Time: 40 minutes / Total Time: 1 hour and 30 minutes

This summertime dish is fabulous served outside on your porch or patio, particularly with some Shishito Peppers (see page 385).

1 Heat the 2 tablespoons of olive oil in a small skillet over medium-high heat. Once hot, add the ginger, onions, garlic, and lemon juice and sauté for about 2 to 3 minutes, or until the garlic is crisp but not browned. Remove from heat and transfer to a small bowl.

2 Rub the chicken breasts with pepper and salt and put them in a resealable plastic bag. Add the ginger-and-onion mixture and press it around the chicken breasts. Seal and let rest at room temperature for 30 minutes.

3 Bring your gas or charcoal grill to medium-high heat.

4 In a small dish, combine the remaining olive oil with the sesame seeds. Set aside.

5 Once the grill is ready, about 425°F with the coals lightly covered with ash, place the chicken on the grill and sprinkle the tops with half of the oiled sesame seeds. Grill the chicken breasts for about 7 minutes. Flip the chicken over and season with the remaining sesame seeds, and then grill for 5 to 6 more minutes. When finished, the chicken breasts should feel springy when poked.

6 Remove and let rest for 5 minutes. Serve warm.

TOOLS

Skillet

INGREDIENTS

2 tablespoons plus ½ teaspoon olive oil

2-inch piece of ginger, peeled and sliced

2 green onions, minced

2 garlic cloves, minced

Juice from ½ lemon

4 boneless chicken breasts, about 1½ to 2 pounds total

Coarsely ground black pepper

Sea salt

3 tablespoons sesame seeds

INGREDIENTS

FOR THE CHICKEN

6 to 8 chicken drumsticks
and wings

3 to 4 tablespoons olive oil

1 yellow onion, minced

2 scallions, minced

Juice from ½ lemon or lime

3 garlic cloves, minced

3 teaspoons garam masala

½ teaspoon dried thyme

1 teaspoon ground turmeric

1 teaspoon cayenne pepper

Coarsely ground black pepper

Sea salt

FOR THE MANGO-AVOCADO SALAD

2 mangoes, cubed

Flesh from 2 large avocados,
chopped

¼ small red onion, coarsely
chopped

2 cups tomatoes, chopped

1 cup basil leaves, thinly sliced

Juice from ½ small lemon or lime

1 tablespoon olive oil

2 teaspoons coarsely ground
black pepper

1 teaspoon sea salt

INDIAN-RUBBED CHICKEN WITH MANGO-AVOCADO SALAD

Makes 4 to 5 servings / Active Time: 40 minutes / Total Time: 2 hours

This dish is simpler than you'd think. Just place the chicken drumsticks over the Mango-Avocado Salad for a delicious and easy dinner.

1 Wash and dry the chicken drumsticks and wings and then rub with olive oil. Let rest at room temperature for about 30 minutes.

2 In a small roasting pan, combine the remaining ingredients for the chicken and spread evenly along the bottom of the pan. Rub the chicken drumsticks and wings with the spices. Set aside and let rest for about 1 hour.

3 A half hour before grilling, bring your gas or charcoal grill to medium heat.

4 Once the grill is ready, at about 400°F with the coals lightly covered with ash, place the drumsticks and wings on the grill. Grill for about 30 minutes, rotating the chicken pieces as they cook.

5 Prepare the salad. Combine the mangoes, avocados, red onion, tomatoes, and basil and stir. Add the lemon or lime juice and olive oil and gently stir. Season with black pepper and sea salt and set aside.

6 Remove the drumsticks and wings from the grill when the skins are crispy and charred. Let rest for 5 minutes and then serve alongside the Mango-Avocado Salad.

SMOKED AND PULLED BBQ CHICKEN SANDWICHES

Makes 4 to 6 servings / Active Time: 40 minutes / Total Time: 2½ to 12½ hours

To get the perfect shredded texture, simply grill the chicken first and then quickly braise it in a vinegar-based BBQ sauce.

1 Combine the ingredients for the rub in a large bowl. Add the chicken breasts and rub the spices over them. Place the bowl in the refrigerator for 2 to 12 hours, the longer the better.

2 One hour before grilling, place the wood chips in a bowl of water and let soak. At the same time, bring your gas or charcoal grill to medium heat. Leave the skillet on the grill while heating so that it develops a faint, smoky flavor.

3 Once the grill is ready, at about 400°F with the coals lightly covered with ash, scatter half of the wood chips over the coals or place them in a smoker box and then place the chicken breasts on the grill. Cover the grill, aligning the air vent away from the wood chips so that their smoke billows around the chicken breasts before escaping. Cook for about 7 to 8 minutes on each side and then remove from grill. Transfer the chicken to a large cutting board, let rest for 5 minutes, and then shred the chicken with two forks. Set aside.

4 Prepare the sauce. Scatter the remaining wood chips over the coals or place them in the smoker box, and then place the clarified butter in the skillet. When hot, add the garlic, onion, and shallot and sauté until the garlic is golden and the onion and shallot are translucent. Add the remaining ingredients and simmer for about 15 minutes, or until the sauce has thickened. Mix in the chicken and reduce heat. Cook for 5 more minutes and then remove from heat.

5 Let the chicken rest for 5 minutes, allowing it to properly absorb the sauce, and then serve on warm buns.

TOOLS

2 to 3 cups hickory or oak wood chips

Cast-iron skillet

Smoker box (for gas grill)

INGREDIENTS

FOR THE RUB

1 teaspoon chili powder

¼ teaspoon cayenne pepper

2 teaspoons Tabasco™

½ teaspoon chipotle powder

FOR THE CHICKEN

2 to 3 pounds skinless, boneless chicken breasts

6 hamburger buns, warmed, for serving

FOR THE BBQ SAUCE

2 tablespoons butter, clarified

4 garlic cloves, minced

½ cup white onion, minced

½ shallot, minced

¾ cup tomatoes, crushed

1 cup apple cider vinegar

2 tablespoons honey

Coarsely ground black pepper

Sea salt

CHICKEN UNDER A BRICK WITH CILANTRO OIL

Makes 4 to 6 servings   /   Active Time: 1 hour   /   Total Time: 2 hours

This is a classic preparation of chicken that involves spatchcocking the whole chicken, and then cooking it with a brick, wrapped in aluminum foil, resting on top. The brick will not only allow for the chicken to be cooked through perfectly but also produce charred, crispy skin.

1   Place the chicken breast side down on a large cutting board. Then, using a strong set of kitchen shears, cut along each side of the backbone and then remove it. Next, flip over the chicken and flatten the breastbone by pressing down with your hands.

2   Rub the oil on the chicken and then season with the black pepper and sea salt. Let the chicken stand at room temperature for 30 minutes. Wrap the bricks in aluminum foil and then bring your gas or charcoal grill to medium heat. When cooking this dish, you want to designate two separate heat sections on the grill, one for direct heat and the other for indirect heat. To do this, simply arrange the coals toward one side of a charcoal grill or turn off one of the burners on a gas grill.

3   Once the grill is ready, at about 400°F with the coals lightly covered with ash, place the chicken breast side down over indirect heat. Lay the foil-wrapped bricks on top of the chicken and grill until the skin is crisp, about 25 to 30 minutes. Next, using tongs or thick oven mitts, remove the bricks from the chicken and set aside. Flip the chicken over and lay the bricks on top. Cover the grill and cook for another 20 minutes until the skin is crisp and a meat thermometer inserted into the thickest part of the thigh reads 160°F.

4   Transfer the chicken to a large cutting board and let rest for 10 to 15 minutes. While the chicken is resting, prepare the oil. Add the cilantro, garlic, and lime juice to a food processer. Puree to a paste and then slowly add the olive oil until you reach the desired consistency.

5   Carve the chicken and lightly drizzle with the Cilantro Oil.

TOOLS

2 bricks

Aluminum foil

Food processor

INGREDIENTS

FOR THE CHICKEN

4- to 5-pound chicken

2 tablespoons olive oil

2 tablespoons coarsely ground black pepper

2 tablespoons sea salt

FOR THE CILANTRO OIL

2 bunches of fresh cilantro, leaves removed

2 garlic cloves, minced

Juice from 1 small lime

¼ to ½ cup olive oil

CHICKEN BREASTS WITH BASIL & CHILI OIL

Makes 4 servings / Active Time: 20 minutes / Total Time: 14 hours

While the chicken itself has a soft taste thanks to the basil, the Chili Oil comes in with a semi-strong burst of heat. To be safe, serve the oil on the side. This preparation works well with the Cubanelle Peppers and Plum Tomatoes (see page 386).

1   Prepare the Chili Oil. Place the chili peppers in a small saucepan over medium-high heat. Lightly toast until the skin is blackened, about 3 to 4 minutes. Remove the chilies and set aside. Next, add the olive oil to the saucepan and cook until warm. Stir in the garlic and coriander and cook for 4 to 5 minutes. Return the chilies and cook for 4 more minutes. Remove and let rest overnight. You can store the chili oil in the refrigerator up to 4 months. Keep in mind that the longer the chili infuses into the oil, the hotter it will be.

2   Prepare the chicken. Place the basil leaves, scallions, garlic, and chili pepper in a large bowl, and then add the olive oil. Add the chicken breasts to the marinade and place in the refrigerator. Let soak for at least 4 hours or overnight.

3   Remove the Chili Oil from the refrigerator and set aside. Also, remove the chicken from the marinade, place on a large cutting board, and let rest at room temperature for 30 minutes to 1 hour.

4   Bring your gas or charcoal grill to medium-high heat. Once the grill is ready, at about 425°F with the coals lightly covered with ash, place the chicken on the grill and cook for about 7 minutes. Flip and grill for another 5 to 6 minutes until finished. The chicken breasts should feel springy when poked.

5   Remove and let rest for 5 minutes. Serve warm with the Chili Oil on the side.

INGREDIENTS

FOR THE CHILI OIL

2 chili peppers of your choice

¾ cup olive oil

1 garlic clove, crushed

1 teaspoon ground coriander

FOR THE CHICKEN

2 cups fresh basil leaves

3 scallions, chopped

2 garlic cloves

1 chili pepper of your choice, stemmed and coarsely chopped

¼ to ½ cup olive oil

4 boneless, skin-on chicken breasts

Coarsely ground black pepper

Sea salt

INGREDIENTS

FOR THE TACOS

¾ cup fresh cilantro, minced

Zest and juice of 2 limes

½ cup olive oil

1 teaspoon red pepper flakes

2 teaspoons coarsely ground black pepper

1 teaspoon sea salt

4 to 5 boneless, skinless chicken breasts

12 to 16 corn tortillas, homemade (see pages 402–3) or store-bought

1 head of iceberg lettuce, leaves removed and shredded, for serving

2 to 3 cups cherry tomatoes, quartered, for serving

½ white onion, chopped, for serving

1 cup Salsa Verde (see pages 238–39), for serving

FOR THE SPICY GUACAMOLE

Flesh from 2 large avocados

Juice from ½ small lime

¼ small white onion, minced

¼ to ½ cup cilantro, chopped

1 jalapeño pepper, stemmed, seeded, and minced

Coarsely ground black pepper

Sea salt

CILANTRO-LIME CHICKEN TACOS WITH SPICY GUACAMOLE

Makes 4 servings / Active Time: 30 minutes / Total Time: 4 to 16 hours

The tanginess of the cilantro and lime juice really enhances the Spicy Guacamole. Serve this on a warm summer night with a red wine sangria for an unforgettable family meal.

1 Prepare the chicken for the tacos. Place the cilantro, lime zest and juice, olive oil, red pepper flakes, black pepper, sea salt, and chicken breasts in a large resealable plastic bag. Rub the marinade around in the bag so that it is evenly distributed across the chicken breasts. Seal, transfer to the refrigerator, and let marinate for at least 2 hours or overnight.

2 Remove the chicken from the refrigerator and place, uncovered, on a large cutting board. Let rest for 30 minutes to 1 hour.

3 A half hour before grilling, bring your gas or charcoal grill to medium heat.

4 Once the grill is ready, about 400°F with the coals lightly covered with ash, place the chicken breasts on the grill and cook for about 7 minutes. When the bottoms seem charred, flip the chicken over and grill for another 5 to 6 minutes. The chicken breasts should feel springy when poked.

5 Transfer the chicken from the grill to a large cutting board and let rest for 10 to 15 minutes, allowing the meat to retain its juices.

6 While the chicken rests, place all of the guacamole ingredients in a large bowl and stir to combine with a pestle or fork. Make sure that medium-sized chunks of avocado remain.

7 Cut the chicken into bite-sized pieces and place into a bowl for serving. Serve with the Spicy Guacamole, corn tortillas, lettuce, tomatoes, onion, and Salsa Verde.

SMOKED GINGER CHICKEN SATAY WITH ALMOND DIPPING SAUCE

Makes 5 servings / Active Time: 30 minutes / Total Time: 2 hours and 30 minutes

The chicken takes center stage when served with this almond-based sauce, a milder substitute for the more traditional peanut sauce.

1   Place all of the ingredients for the chicken into a large resealable plastic bag and seal, making sure that the marinade covers the chicken strips. Rub the marinade around the chicken in the bag and transfer to the refrigerator. Let marinate for 2 hours.

2   In a medium bowl, add the wood chips and cover with water. Let soak for 1 hour.

3   Bring your gas or charcoal grill to medium heat.

4   Remove the chicken strips from the marinade and pierce with the skewers.

5   Combine all of the ingredients for the sauce in a small saucepan and bring to a boil over medium-high heat. Cook for about 3 to 4 minutes until the sauce turns golden brown. Remove from heat and cover with aluminum foil.

6   Once the grill is ready, about 400°F with the coals lightly covered with ash, scatter the wood chips over the coals or place them in a smoker box. Wait a few minutes for the smoke to build, and then place the skewered chicken strips on the grill. Cover the grill, aligning the vent away from the heat so that the smoke billows over the chicken strips, and cook for about 4 minutes on each side.

7   Remove from heat and serve alongside the warm Almond Dipping Sauce.

VARIATION

Consider serving with a Spicy Peanut Sauce. For a Spicy Peanut Sauce, combine ½ cup chicken broth, 2 tablespoons peanut butter, 1½ tablespoons soy sauce, 2 teaspoons honey, 1 teaspoon Sriracha, and 1 minced garlic clove in a saucepan. Bring to a boil, cover the saucepan, and reduce the heat so that the sauce continues to cook at a simmer for about 5 minutes. Remove from heat, transfer to a bowl, and serve.

TOOLS

2 to 3 cups hickory or oak wood chips

Skewers

Saucepan

Smoker box (for gas grill)

INGREDIENTS

FOR THE CHICKEN SATAY

10 boneless, skinless chicken thighs, cut into thin strips

1- to 2-inch piece of ginger, peeled and thinly sliced

2 tablespoons sesame seeds

1 large shallot, minced

3 garlic cloves

1 teaspoon ground coriander

1 chili pepper of your choice, stemmed

2 teaspoons coarsely ground black pepper

1 teaspoon sea salt

¼ cup olive oil

FOR THE ALMOND DIPPING SAUCE

½ cup almond butter

1½ cups coconut milk

Juice from 1 lime wedge

1 tablespoon fish sauce

½ teaspoon coarsely ground black pepper

½ teaspoon sea salt

LEMON AND GARLIC CHICKEN

Makes 4 to 6 servings / Active Time: 1 hour and 15 minutes / Total Time: 1 hour and 30 minutes

When you're serving a large group and pressed for time, the simple elegance of this classic dish always impresses.

1 Bring your gas or charcoal grill to medium heat.

2 Place the chicken in a large roasting pan and season its cavity generously with black pepper and sea salt. Take 5 of the lemon halves and put them in the cavity, gently squeezing them while doing so. Rub the remaining lemon half across the chicken, squeezing it lightly to release its juice. Discard this half and then fill the cavity with the garlic, thyme, and rosemary. Tie the legs together with the butcher's twine and let rest for 15 minutes.

3 Take 4 tablespoons of the olive oil and massage it over the chicken's skin. Season the outside with additional pepper and salt.

4 Once the grill is ready, at about 400°F with the coals lightly covered with ash, place the chicken on the grill, breast side up. Cover the grill and cook for about 40 minutes. Before flipping the chicken over, brush the top of the chicken with the remaining tablespoon of olive oil. Turn over and cook for about 15 more minutes, until the skin is crisp and a meat thermometer reads 165°F when inserted into the thickest part of the thigh.

5 Remove the chicken from the grill and place on a large cutting board. Let the chicken rest at room temperature for 10 minutes before carving. Serve warm.

NOTE: *For a bit more flavor, heavily rinse the chicken's cavity with a couple cups of orange juice and salt before placing the lemons, garlic, thyme, and rosemary inside.*

TOOLS

1 to 2 feet butcher's twine

INGREDIENTS

4- to 5-pound chicken

Coarsely ground black pepper

Sea salt

3 lemons, halved

1 head of garlic, halved

1 bunch of thyme

1 bunch of rosemary

5 tablespoons olive oil

SPICY LIME CHICKEN BREASTS

Makes 4 servings / Active Time: 15 minutes / Total Time: 1 hour and 15 minutes

To add another layer of flavor to this recipe, simply add ¾ cup of cubed mango to the marinade before adding the chicken.

1 In a large resealable bag or a large bowl, place all of the marinade ingredients. Whisk until thoroughly combined. Next, place the chicken breasts in the marinade, cover or seal the container, transfer to the refrigerator, and let the chicken marinate for approximately 1 hour.

2 Bring your gas or charcoal grill to medium heat.

3 Once the grill is ready, at about 400°F with the coals lightly covered with ash, place the chicken directly on the grill and season the tops with black pepper and sea salt. Grill for about 7 to 9 minutes per side. When the chicken is cooked through and juicy, remove the chicken from the grill and let stand at room temperature for 5 minutes before serving.

INGREDIENTS

FOR THE MARINADE

3 tablespoons extra virgin olive oil

2 teaspoons chili powder

1 teaspoon garlic powder

1 teaspoon onion powder

1 teaspoon honey

Juice from 2 limes

FOR THE CHICKEN

4 boneless, skinless chicken breasts

Coarsely ground black pepper

Sea salt

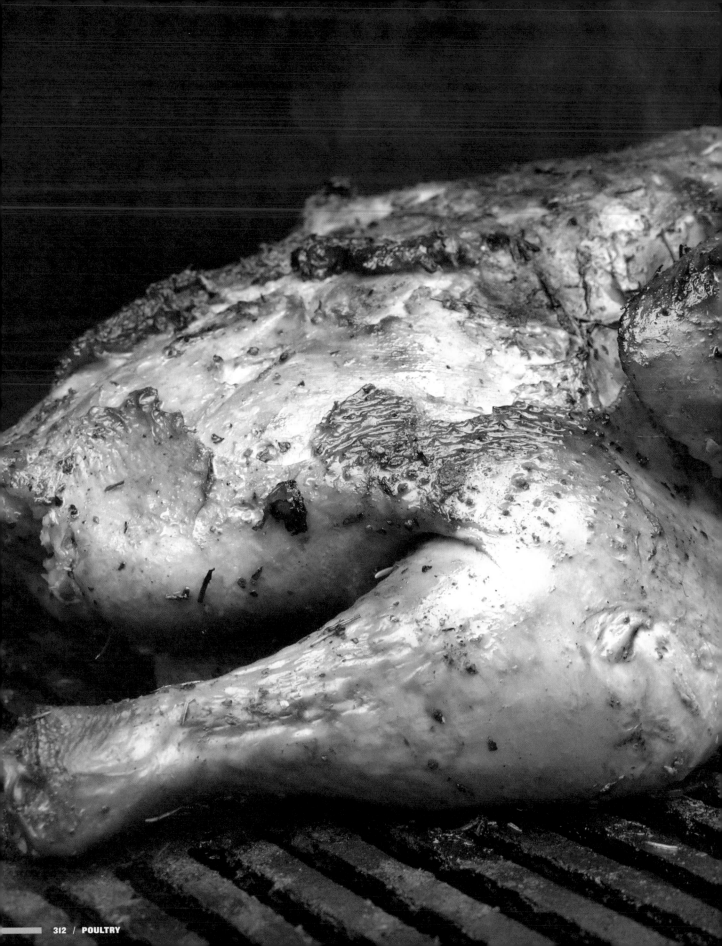

BRINED TURKEY

Makes 8 to 10 servings / Active Time: 3 hours / Total Time: 9 to 24 hours

Brining and grilling poultry go hand in hand, as the brining allows the meat to retain its juices and stay moist. To brine thoroughly, the bird must soak in a mixture of water and kosher salt for up to 12 hours, the longer the better. Serve with Cranberry Sauce (see page 314).

1. In a large stockpot, add the turkey and cover with the 8 cups of water and ½ cup of kosher salt. If you need to add water to cover the turkey, make sure to increase the amount of kosher salt. Let the turkey brine at room temperature for 6 to 12 hours.

2. Remove the turkey and pat dry. Grab the orange halves and squeeze over the turkey and inside its cavity. Next, rub the clarified butter over the turkey skin and season with the rosemary and coarsely ground black pepper.

3. Bring your gas or charcoal grill to medium-low heat and designate two separate heat sections on the grill, one for direct heat and the other for indirect. To do this, simply arrange the coals toward one side of a charcoal grill or turn off one of the burners on a gas grill.

4. Once the grill is ready, at about 350°F with the coals lightly covered with ash, place the turkey over indirect heat and grill for about 2 hours and 45 minutes. While grilling, you want to replenish the coals and flip the turkey every 45 minutes. Insert a meat thermometer into the thickest part of the thigh. When the turkey is finished, the thermometer should read 165°F.

5. Remove the turkey from the grill and cover with aluminum foil. Let rest for 45 minutes to 1 hour before carving.

INGREDIENTS

12- to 14-pound turkey

8 cups cold water, plus more as needed

½ cup kosher salt, plus more as needed

2 oranges, halved

2 tablespoons butter, clarified

Leaves from ½ sprig of rosemary

Coarsely ground black pepper

CAJUN TURKEY WITH CRANBERRY SAUCE

Makes 8 to 10 servings / Active Time: 3 hours / Total Time: 16 to 24 hours

Slice the turkey completely after grilling, then set aside the extra meat for turkey and cranberry sauce sandwiches the next day!

1 Prepare the Cranberry Sauce. Combine the cranberries, honey, orange juice, and lemon juice in a saucepan over medium heat. Simmer for about 15 minutes, until the sauce thickens and the berries break apart. Transfer to a bowl and refrigerate overnight.

2 In a large stockpot, add the turkey and cover with the 8 cups of water. Add the kosher salt. If you need to add more water to fully cover the turkey, make sure to increase the amount of kosher salt. Let the turkey brine at room temperature for 6 to 12 hours.

3 Remove the turkey from the brine and pat dry. Place the remaining ingredients, except for the butter, in a small bowl and stir to combine. Spoon the clarified butter over the turkey and then apply the mixture in the bowl to the turkey. Let stand at room temperature for 1 to 2 hours.

4 Bring your gas or charcoal grill to medium-low heat and designate two separate heat sections on the grill, one for direct heat and the other for indirect. To do this, simply arrange the coals toward one side of a charcoal grill or turn off one of the burners on a gas grill.

5 Once the grill is ready, at about 350°F with the coals lightly covered with ash, place the turkey over indirect heat and grill for about 2 to 2½ hours. While grilling, you want to replenish the coals and flip the turkey every 45 minutes. To check for doneness, insert a meat thermometer into the thickest part of the thigh. When finished, the turkey should be at 165°F.

6 Remove the turkey from the grill and cover with aluminum foil. Let rest for 45 minutes to 1 hour before carving. Serve alongside the Cranberry Sauce.

TOOLS

Saucepan

INGREDIENTS

FOR THE CRANBERRY SAUCE

4 cups raw cranberries

⅓ cup honey

½ cup orange juice

Juice from ½ small lemon

FOR THE TURKEY

12- to 14-pound turkey

8 cups cold water, plus more as needed

½ cup kosher salt, plus more as needed

2 tablespoons onion powder

2 tablespoons paprika

1 tablespoon cayenne pepper

1 tablespoon garlic powder

1 tablespoon ground oregano

1 tablespoon dried thyme

1 tablespoon coarsely ground black pepper

1 tablespoon sea salt

2 tablespoons butter, clarified

CIDER-GLAZED CORNISH HENS

Makes 4 servings / Active Time: 1 hour / Total Time: 4 hours and 30 minutes

This dish is perfect for a cool fall evening. Be sure to spatchcock the hens beforehand, as this will allow the breasts to cook evenly.

1 Season the Cornish hens with coarsely ground black pepper and sea salt. Combine the olive oil, thyme, tarragon, and lemon juice in a small bowl and then place the Cornish hens into the mixture. Let marinate at room temperature for 2 to 4 hours, turning the hens over every 30 minutes so that the marinade coats them evenly.

2 Bring your gas or charcoal grill to medium heat and designate two separate heat sections on the grill, one for direct heat and the other for indirect. To do this, simply arrange the coals toward one side of a charcoal grill or turn off one of the burners on a gas grill.

3 While waiting for the grill, combine the ingredients for the glaze in a small saucepan and place over medium-high heat. Bring the glaze to a boil and cook until it has reduced to approximately ½ cup, about 10 minutes. Remove from heat and transfer to a small bowl.

4 Once the grill is ready, at 400°F with the coals lightly covered with ash, brush the glaze over the Cornish hens. Then, place the birds breast side down over direct heat and cook for 3 minutes. When the skin is slightly crispy, flip the hens over and place over indirect heat. Cook for another 25 minutes, frequently basting with the remaining glaze, until the hens are cooked through.

5 Remove the hens from the grill and transfer to a large cutting board. Let rest for 5 to 10 minutes before serving.

TOOLS

Saucepan

INGREDIENTS

FOR THE CORNISH HENS

4 (1¼ pound) Cornish hens, spatchcocked (see Step 1 on page 301)

Coarsely ground black pepper

Sea salt

¼ cup olive oil

Leaves from 1 sprig of thyme

Leaves from 1 sprig of tarragon

Juice from ½ small lemon

FOR THE CIDER GLAZE

1 cup apple cider with no added sugar

1 tablespoon honey

¼ cup butter, clarified

QUAIL WITH CITRUS SPINACH SALAD

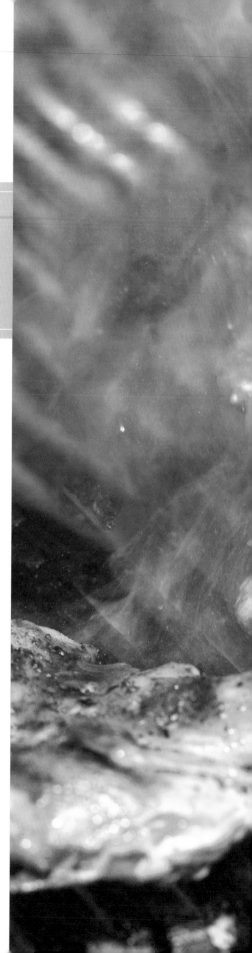

Makes 4 servings / Active Time: 20 minutes / Total Time: 2 hours

Pair this dish with a glass of crisp white wine and you've got yourself a lovely springtime meal.

1. Coat the quail with the olive oil and then season with black pepper and sea salt. Let stand at room temperature for 1 to 1½ hours.

2. Prepare the salad. Add the ½ cup olive oil, vinegar, lime juice, orange juice, and shallot to a small jar, and then season with salt and pepper. In a large bowl, add the spinach, tomatoes, currants, sunflower seeds, and sesame seeds, toss to combine, and set aside. Next, in a small frying pan, heat the 1 tablespoon of olive oil and add the pine nuts. Toast until the pine nuts are brown. Remove from heat and stir them into the large bowl.

3. Bring your gas or charcoal grill to medium-high heat.

4. Once the grill is ready, at about 425°F with the coals lightly covered with ash, place the quail breast side up and cook until the skin is lightly browned, about 5 minutes. Flip the quail over and grill for 2 more minutes. When finished, transfer the quail to a large cutting board and let rest for 5 to 10 minutes.

5. Add the vinaigrette to the salad and toss to combine. Divide the salad between the plates and top with the quail.

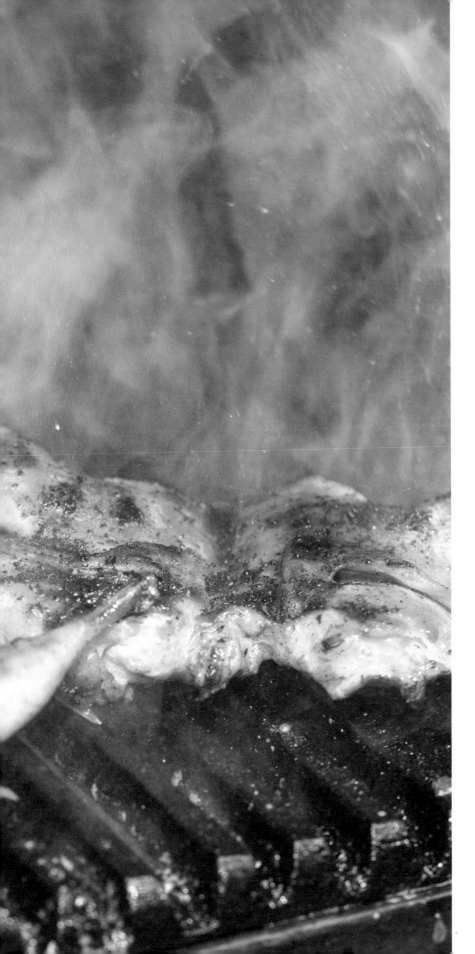

TOOLS

Frying pan

INGREDIENTS

FOR THE QUAIL

4 to 6 quail, spatchcocked
(see Step 1 on page 301)

2 tablespoons olive oil

Coarsely ground black pepper

Sea salt

FOR THE CITRUS SPINACH SALAD

½ cup plus 1 tablespoon olive oil

4 tablespoons white wine vinegar

Juice from ½ small lime

Juice from ¼ orange

1 small shallot, minced

Coarsely ground black pepper

Sea salt

4 cups baby spinach

½ to 1 cup cherry tomatoes, quartered

4 tablespoons currants

3 tablespoons sunflower seeds

2 tablespoons sesame seeds

½ cup pine nuts

TERIYAKI CHICKEN KEBABS

Makes 4 to 6 servings / Active Time: 20 minutes / Total Time: 50 minutes

It's hard to determine what's the best part of this meal: the succulent kebabs, or the easy cleanup.

1 Bring your gas or charcoal grill to medium-high heat.

2 Divide the zucchini, peppers, onion, and chicken between the bamboo skewers.

3 Once the grill is ready, at about 425°F with the coals lightly covered with ash, place the kebabs on the grill. Grill for about 8 to 12 minutes while basting with the Teriyaki Marinade.

4 Once the chicken is tender and juicy, remove the kebabs from the grill, season with pepper and salt, and serve immediately.

TOOLS

15 to 20 bamboo skewers, soaked in water

INGREDIENTS

1 zucchini, cut into 1-inch chunks

3 bell peppers, cut into 1-inch chunks

1 white onion, cut into 1-inch chunks

2 boneless, skinless chicken breasts, sliced into 1-inch cubes

1 cup Teriyaki Marinade (see page 125)

Coarsely ground black pepper

Sea salt

CHICKEN TACOS WITH CHARRED CHERRY TOMATO SALSA

Makes 4 to 6 servings / Active Time: 20 minutes / Total Time: 4 to 5 hours

The key to successfully making this recipe is organization. You want to make sure you have enough room on the grill for braising the chicken in a Dutch oven and making the salsa in a cast-iron skillet.

1 Bring your gas or charcoal grill to medium-low heat. Place a cast-iron skillet on the grill while it heats, as this will be used for the salsa.

2 While waiting for your grill to heat up, place all of the taco ingredients, except for those designated for serving, in a bowl and mix thoroughly until the chicken breasts are evenly coated. Transfer the chicken to a large Dutch oven and cover.

3 Once the grill is ready, at about 325°F with the coals lightly covered with ash, place the Dutch oven on one side of the grill and cover the grill. You will slowly cook the chicken for 3 to 4 hours, so make sure you tend the grill and keep a close eye on the temperature.

4 Right after the chicken begins cooking in the Dutch oven, prepare the salsa. Combine the olive oil, cherry tomatoes, onion, garlic cloves, and jalapeño peppers in a bowl. Next, transfer the mixture to the heated cast-iron skillet and grill for about 20 minutes, stirring every now and then until tomatoes are charred. Once charred, transfer the contents of the skillet to a food processor along with the remaining ingredients. Pulse until smooth, and then cover for at least 2 hours while the chicken continues to cook.

5 After 3 hours, open the Dutch oven and use a fork to check the chicken. When finished, the chicken should fall apart easily. While the chicken usually takes closer to 4 hours to reach this point, make sure to check regularly after 3 hours to avoid overcooking.

6 Remove the Dutch oven from the grill and, using two forks, shred the chicken.

7 Serve the with the salsa, corn tortillas, cilantro, jalapeños, and onion.

VARIATION

Grilled scallions make for another wonderful topping for these tacos.

TOOLS

Dutch oven

Cast-iron skillet

INGREDIENTS

FOR THE CHICKEN TACOS

3 pounds boneless, skinless chicken breasts

2 teaspoons ground cumin

1 teaspoon all-purpose seasoning

2 garlic cloves, minced

1 tablespoon chili powder

1 tablespoon brown sugar

Juice from 1 large lime

¼ cup cilantro, chopped, plus more for serving

1 teaspoon coarsely ground black pepper

1 teaspoon sea salt

15 to 20 corn tortillas, homemade (see pages 402–3) or store-bought, for serving

2 jalapeño peppers, chopped, for serving

1 onion, chopped, for serving

FOR THE SALSA

2 tablespoons extra virgin olive oil

1 pint cherry tomatoes

1 yellow onion, chopped

6 garlic cloves, crushed

2 jalapeño peppers, diced

½ cup cilantro leaves

Juice from 1 lime

1 teaspoon ground cumin

Coarsely ground black pepper

Sea salt

SEAFOOD & SHELLFISH

SEAFOOD & SHELLFISH

MODERN SCIENCE AND EARLY CIVILIZATION can find common ground on one thing: micronutrients such as omega-3s, which are commonly found in seafoods, are essential to brain development. That might explain why so many early peoples were coastal dwellers, or why seafood has become a staple of diets around the world.

The healthiest—and tastiest—way to make seafood and shellfish part of your diet is to mix up your selections, just as you would with fresh fruits and vegetables. This chapter includes recipes for salmon, tuna steaks, mahi-mahi, red snapper, swordfish, scallops, oysters, haddock, trout, flounder, shrimp, mussels, striped bass, and—for a grand finale—a grilled seafood stew, to help you explore the wonderful world of seafood dishes. If you are a fan of milder seafoods, the Salmon over Red Bell Peppers (see page 329) is right up your alley. If you are looking for a punchier seafood dish, check out the Red Snapper with Chili-Tomato Sauce (see pages 336–37). And make sure to take advantage of your regional seafood providers to support local fishing and help expand your horizons. Most of these recipes can be made with a variety of fish, so explore the full range of options that the ocean has to offer.

SALMON OVER RED BELL PEPPERS

Makes 4 servings / Active Time: 25 minutes / Total Time: 50 minutes

A classic grilled fillet of salmon is a dish that can often stand by itself. Even so, serving it over some grilled red bell peppers complements the mellow taste of the salmon and brings out the subtle flavors in the vegetables.

1 Place the salmon on a large platter and coat evenly with olive oil, black pepper, and sea salt. Take the lemon half and squeeze it over the salmon. Let rest at room temperature.

2 A half hour before cooking, place a cast-iron skillet on your gas or charcoal grill and bring to medium heat. Leave the grill covered while heating, as it will add a faint smoky flavor to the skillet.

3 Once the grill is ready, at about 400°F with the coals lightly covered with ash, add the red bell peppers to the cast-iron skillet and let cook, turning occasionally, until the peppers are nearly charred and wrinkled, about 20 minutes. Remove the peppers and let cool.

4 Place the salmon on the grill and cook for about 5 to 6 minutes per side, until the fish is flaky when pierced with a fork. Transfer to a cutting board and let rest for 5 to 10 minutes.

5 Take the peppers and remove the stems and seeds. Next, cut the peppers into long strips and place them in a medium bowl. Add the olive oil, balsamic vinegar, and thyme, stir to combine, and serve alongside the salmon fillets.

TOOLS

Cast-iron skillet

INGREDIENTS

FOR THE SALMON

4 (4 inch) salmon fillets

2 tablespoons olive oil

Coarsely ground black pepper

Sea salt

½ lemon

FOR THE PEPPERS

4 red bell peppers

2 tablespoons olive oil

1 teaspoon balsamic vinegar

Leaves from 1 sprig of thyme

SPICED HONEY SALMON

Makes 4 servings / Active Time: 25 minutes / Total Time: 1 hour and 10 minutes

Cutting the sweetness of the honey with aromatic garlic goes wonderfully with the fresh, light taste of the salmon. Serve with Charred Sweet Potatoes (see page 382) for a filling lunch or a light dinner.

1 Combine the honey, chives, hot water, garlic clove, and lemon juice in a food processor and blend to a paste. Remove the paste from the processor and coat the salmon fillets evenly with the mixture. Season with black pepper and sea salt. Set aside and let marinate for at least 30 minutes.

2 Preheat your gas or charcoal grill to medium-high heat.

3 Once the grill is ready, at about 425°F with the coals lightly covered with ash, place the salmon fillets on the grill and cook for about 4 minutes per side, until the fish is flaky when pierced with a fork.

4 Transfer the fillets to a cutting board and let rest for 5 to 10 minutes before serving.

TOOLS

Food processor

INGREDIENTS

4 tablespoons honey

1 tablespoon fresh chives, chopped

2 teaspoons hot water

1 large garlic clove

Juice from ½ small lemon

4 (4 inch) salmon fillets

Coarsely ground black pepper

Sea salt

CITRUS-GLAZED SALMON

Makes 4 servings / **Active Time: 35 minutes** / **Total Time: 1 hour**

A friend of mine makes the most outstanding version of this dish with a portable grill in her small Manhattan apartment. Salmon and citrus were a match made in heaven, as the tanginess of the juice contrasts the subtle sweetness of the fish.

1 Combine all of the ingredients except the salmon fillets in a small saucepan and bring to a boil. Stir continually and cook until the sauce has reduced to a thick syrup, about 15 minutes. Remove from heat and let stand.

2 Preheat your gas or charcoal grill to medium-high heat.

3 Season both sides of the salmon fillets with black pepper and sea salt.

4 Once the grill is ready, at about 425°F with the coals lightly covered with ash, place the salmon fillets on the grill and cook for about 3 to 4 minutes per side, using a brush to apply the glaze to the salmon while cooking.

5 When the salmon is flaky when pierced with a fork, remove the fillets from the grill and serve with the remaining glaze on the side.

TOOLS

Saucepan

INGREDIENTS

Juice from 1 lemon

Juice from 1 large orange

Juice from 2 limes

¼ cup Chicken Stock
(see page 47)

2 garlic cloves, minced

2 tablespoons soy sauce

2 tablespoons orange marmalade

2 tablespoons brown sugar

1 tablespoon unsalted butter

Coarsely ground black pepper

Sea salt

4 salmon fillets, each about
1 to 1½ inches thick

SEARED TUNA STEAKS WITH DILL AIOLI

Makes 4 servings / Active Time: 25 minutes / Total Time: 50 minutes

Seared tuna steaks are always a treat on a warm summer evening, since they are great chilled or right off the grill.

1 Rub the tuna steaks with the olive oil and season with black pepper and sea salt. Let rest at room temperature while you prepare the grill.

2 Bring your gas or charcoal grill to high heat.

3 While waiting for the grill to heat up, combine the dill, parsley, lemon juice, and garlic clove in a small bowl and whisk together. While whisking, slowly incorporate the olive oil and season with sea salt. Set aside or chill in the refrigerator. If you want a lighter aioli, combine the initial ingredients in a blender and then slowly add the olive oil.

4 Once the grill is ready, at about 450°F with the coals lightly covered with ash, brush the grate with a little olive oil. Tuna steaks should always be cooked between rare and medium-rare; anything more will be tough and dry. To accomplish a perfect searing, place the tuna steaks directly over the hottest part of the grill and sear for about 2 minutes per side. The tuna should be raw in the middle (cook 2½ to 3 minutes per side for medium-rare).

5 Transfer the tuna steaks to a large cutting board and let rest for 5 to 10 minutes. Slice against the grain and then serve with the Dill Aioli on the side.

INGREDIENTS

FOR THE TUNA

4 fresh tuna steaks, each about 2 inches thick

2 tablespoon olive oil, plus more for brushing the grill

Coarsely ground black pepper

Sea salt

FOR THE DILL AIOLI

Leaves from 10 sprigs of dill, minced

Leaves from 10 sprigs of parsley, minced

Juice from ¼ small lemon

1 garlic clove, minced

¾ cup olive oil

Sea salt

TOOLS

Cast-iron skillet

INGREDIENTS

FOR THE RED SNAPPER

4 red snapper fillets, skin-on and each about 1½ to 2 inches thick

2 tablespoons olive oil

2 teaspoons red pepper flakes (optional)

Coarsely ground black pepper

Sea salt

FOR THE CHILI-TOMATO SAUCE

2 chili peppers of your choice

2 tablespoons olive oil

1 small shallot, minced

2 garlic cloves, minced

2 pounds large tomatoes, crushed

¼ cup fresh cilantro, minced

1 tablespoon flat-leaf parsley, minced

2 tablespoons fresh chives, minced

Coarsely ground black pepper

Sea salt

RED SNAPPER WITH CHILI-TOMATO SAUCE

Makes 4 servings / Active Time: 25 minutes / Total Time: 1 hour

Red snapper grills well because of its firm texture and mild taste. It's also a perfect vehicle for spicy components like the Chili-Tomato Sauce.

1 Rub the snapper fillets with olive oil and then season with the red pepper flakes (if desired), black pepper, and sea salt. Let stand at room temperature while preheating the grill.

2 A half hour before cooking, place a cast-iron skillet on your gas or charcoal grill and bring to medium heat. Leave the grill covered while heating, as it will add a faint smoky flavor to the skillet.

3 Once the grill is ready, at about 400°F with the coals lightly covered with ash, add the chili peppers to the skillet and cook until the chilies are charred and wrinkled. Remove from pan and transfer to a small cutting board. Let cool and then stem the chilies. Finely chop them and set aside.

4 Add the olive oil to the cast-iron skillet. When hot, add the shallot and garlic and cook until the shallot is translucent and the garlic is golden, about 2 minutes. Add the finely chopped chilies to the pan and cook for 1 minute. Stir in the tomatoes and cook until they have broken down. Stir in the cilantro, parsley, and chives and cook for a few more minutes. Season with pepper and salt and transfer to a bowl. While the sauce is still hot, mash with a fork and cover with aluminum foil.

5 Place the seasoned snapper fillets on the grill. Cover the grill and cook for about 3 minutes per side. When finished, the fillets should be opaque in the center and should easily tear when pierced with a fork. Transfer to a cutting board and peel back the skin. Let rest 5 to 10 minutes and serve on beds of the Chili-Tomato Sauce.

LIME MAHI-MAHI AND GREEN BEANS WITH PROSCIUTTO & PINE NUTS

Makes 4 servings / Active Time: 45 minutes / Total Time: 2 hours and 30 minutes

Because the mahi-mahi has such a delicate taste, it works with nearly any side or marinade. Here, it acts as the ideal partner for the prosciutto and pine nuts.

1 Prepare the mahi-mahi. In a medium roasting pan, combine the olive oil, lime juice, garlic, red pepper flakes, and cayenne pepper and mix thoroughly. Place the mahi-mahi fillets in the marinade and let stand at room temperature for 1 to 2 hours, flipping them over once.

2 A half hour before cooking, place a cast-iron skillet on your gas or charcoal grill and bring to medium heat. Leave the grill covered while heating, as it will add a faint smoky flavor to the skillet.

3 Once the grill is ready, at about 400°F with the coals lightly covered with ash, add 2 tablespoons olive oil to the skillet. Wait until it is very hot, and then add the prosciutto and sear until browned. Next, stir in the pine nuts and toast for about 3 minutes. Stir in the garlic and green beans and top with the lemon juice. Season generously with black pepper and sea salt and cook until the green beans are charred and blistered, about 10 minutes.

4 While the green beans cook, remove the mahi-mahi fillets from the marinade and place directly over the heat source. Cover the grill and cook for about 4 to 5 minutes per side, until the fillets are flaky and moist when touched with a fork.

5 Remove the fillets and green beans from the grill, season with pepper and salt, and serve immediately.

TOOLS

Cast-iron skillet

INGREDIENTS

FOR THE MAHI-MAHI

½ cup olive oil

Juice from ½ small lime

1 garlic clove, minced

1 teaspoon red pepper flakes

½ teaspoon cayenne pepper

4 mahi-mahi fillets

Coarsely ground black pepper

Sea salt

FOR THE GREEN BEANS

2 tablespoons olive oil

3 oz. prosciutto, sliced into cubes

¼ cup pine nuts

2 garlic cloves, minced

2 to 3 pounds green beans, ends trimmed

Juice from ¼ small lemon

Coarsely ground black pepper

Sea salt

LEMON AND BASIL SWORDFISH STEAKS WITH CITRUS SALSA

Makes 4 servings / Active Time: 40 minutes / Total Time: 1 hour and 45 minutes

Swordfish is often considered a meat lover's fish, but when it is paired with this Citrus Salsa anyone can get onboard.

INGREDIENTS

FOR THE SWORDFISH

Juice from ½ lemon

¼ cup fresh basil leaves

1 garlic clove, minced

½ cup olive oil, plus more for brushing the grill

4 swordfish steaks, each 1¼ to 1¾ inches thick

Coarsely ground black pepper

Sea salt

FOR THE CITRUS SALSA

1 cup ripe pineapple, diced

¼ cup fresh cucumber, diced

¼ cup ripe mango, diced

1 small shallot, chopped

2 tablespoons red bell pepper, diced

1 tablespoon fresh cilantro, minced

Juice from ¼ small lime

Dash of Tabasco™

Coarsely ground black pepper

Sea salt

1   In a medium bowl, combine the lemon juice, basil leaves, and garlic. Whisk in the olive oil and then let the marinade infuse for 1 hour. Next, rub this over the swordfish steaks and then season with pepper and sea salt. Let stand at room temperature while you prepare the grill and the Citrus Salsa.

2   Bring your gas or charcoal grill to high heat.

3   While the grill heats up, prepare the salsa. Combine the pineapple, cucumber, mango, shallot, red bell pepper, and cilantro in a large bowl. Stir in the lime juice and Tabasco™ and then season with black pepper and sea salt. Transfer the bowl to the refrigerator and let chill.

4   Once the grill is ready, at about 450°F with the coals lightly covered with ash, brush the grate with a little olive oil. Place the swordfish steaks on the grill and then grill for about 3 to 4 minutes per side, until the fish is opaque.

5   Remove the steaks from the grill and place on a large cutting board. Let stand for 5 to 10 minutes and then serve alongside the Citrus Salsa.

PEACH SCALLOPS WITH BASIL-CILANTRO PUREE

Makes 4 to 6 servings / Active Time: 45 minutes / Total Time: 2 hours and 20 minutes

Although they seem small, scallops are extremely filling and so do not require a large side to accompany them. A small salad or some Charred Scallions (see page 389) will do the trick.

1. In a large bowl, combine the peaches and olive oil. Let rest for about 30 minutes, until the juices from the peaches cover the bottom of the bowl.

2. Next, season the scallops with the lemon juice, black pepper, and sea salt and then place them in the peach mixture, making sure that most of them are covered. Let the scallops marinate in the refrigerator for 1 to 1½ hours.

3. Bring your gas or charcoal grill to medium heat, designating 2 sections: one for direct heat and the other for indirect. To do so, simply pile the coals on one side of a charcoal grill or turn off one of the burners on a gas grill.

4. Prepare the puree. Place the cilantro, basil, parsley, garlic, and jalapeño in a small food processor. Blend into a thick paste, and then gradually add the lime juice and olive oil until you reach the desired consistency. Season with black pepper and sea salt, remove the mixture from the food processor, and set aside.

5. Once the grill is ready, at about 400°F with the coals lightly covered with ash, place the scallops over indirect heat. Cover the grill and cook for about 5 to 6 minutes, flipping once, until the scallops are firm and lightly charred. To check for doneness, insert a fork into the center. If it comes out cold, cook for another minute or so; if it comes out warm, remove the scallops from the grill.

6. Let the scallops rest on a cutting board for 5 minutes and then divide between the plates. Drizzle the Basil-Cilantro Puree over the scallops and serve the rest on the side.

VARIATION

For additional heat, use 2 tablespoons minced habanero pepper instead of the jalapeño in the puree.

INGREDIENTS

FOR THE SCALLOPS

4 large, ripe peaches, pitted and cut into ¼-inch cubes

2 tablespoons olive oil

15 (U10 or U15) scallops

Juice from 1 lemon wedge

Coarsely ground black pepper

Sea salt

FOR THE BASIL-CILANTRO PUREE

½ cup cilantro leaves

½ cup basil leaves

2 tablespoons flat-leaf parsley leaves

2 garlic cloves, minced

2 tablespoons jalapeño pepper, minced

Juice from ½ small lime

¼ cup olive oil

Coarsely ground black pepper

Sea salt

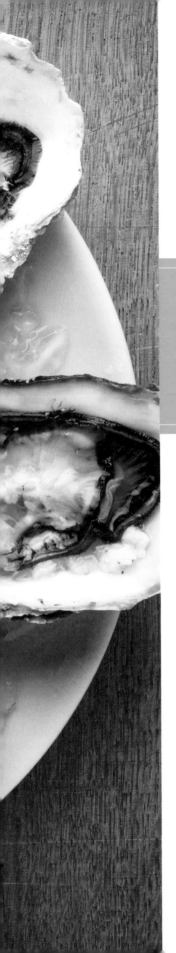

OYSTERS WITH SHALLOT MIGNONETTE

Makes 5 to 6 servings / Active Time: 10 minutes / Total Time: 30 to 45 minutes

Oysters are light and perfect for socializing, particularly when paired with this Shallot Mignonette. They work as a main course, lunch, or even a light snack.

INGREDIENTS

24 oysters

½ cup red wine vinegar

2 tablespoons shallot, minced

½ habanero pepper, seeded and minced (optional)

1 teaspoon flat-leaf parsley, minced

Coarsely ground black pepper

Sea salt

1 lemon, sliced into small wedges, for serving

1   Carefully shuck the oysters and store them in the refrigerator.

2   To make the mignonette, combine the red wine vinegar, minced shallot, habanero (if desired), and parsley in a small bowl and season with black pepper and sea salt. Transfer the bowl to the refrigerator and let the mixture infuse for 30 to 45 minutes.

3   Remove the oysters from the refrigerator and serve on a platter over finely crushed ice. Pour the mignonette into a small bowl and serve with lemon wedges.

SEARED LEMON HADDOCK WITH BASIL-WALNUT PESTO

Makes 4 servings / Active Time: 20 minutes / Total Time: 40 minutes

Haddock is occasionally referred to as the "poor man's lobster," but when paired with the Basil-Walnut Pesto, it wants for nothing.

1. Place the haddock fillets in a small baking pan and then add the olive oil. Season the fillets with black pepper, sea salt, and the lemon juice. Let rest at room temperature while preheating the grill.

2. A half hour before cooking, place a cast-iron skillet on your gas or charcoal grill and bring to medium heat. Leave the grill covered while heating, as it will add a faint smoky flavor to the skillet.

3. Prepare the pesto while the grill heats. Puree the walnuts, basil, cilantro, and garlic cloves in a food processor. When you have a thick paste, slowly blend in the olive oil until it reaches the desired consistency. Remove from food processor, season with black pepper and salt, and set aside.

4. Once the grill is ready, at about 400°F with the coals lightly covered with ash, place the fillets in the skillet and sear for about 5 minutes. Once the fillets have browned, turn and cook for 1 to 2 more minutes, until the fish is opaque through the center.

5. Transfer the haddock fillets to a cutting board and let rest, uncovered, for 5 to 10 minutes. Serve with the Basil-Walnut Pesto.

TOOLS

Cast-iron skillet

Food processor

INGREDIENTS

FOR THE HADDOCK

4 (½ pound) haddock fillets

¼ cup olive oil

Coarsely ground black pepper

Sea salt

Juice from ½ lemon

FOR THE BASIL-WALNUT PESTO

½ cup walnuts

Leaves from 1 bunch of basil

1 tablespoon cilantro leaves

2 garlic cloves

½ cup olive oil

Coarsely ground black pepper

Sea salt

TROUT WITH GARLIC AND HERBS

Makes 4 servings / Active Time: 35 minutes / Total Time: 1 hour and 10 minutes

The tenderness of a grilled trout fillet often depends on the type of water it lived in. While cold-water trout will be more tender than lake trout, they are both equally delicious when served with garlic, rosemary, thyme, and sage.

1 Place the olive oil in a small saucepan and warm over medium-high heat. When hot, stir in the garlic and cook until golden, about 2 minutes. Stir in the white wine vinegar, lemon juice, rosemary, sage, and thyme and simmer for 1 minute. Remove the pan from heat and let infuse for 30 minutes.

2 Place the trout fillets in a large baking dish and cover with the garlic-and-herb oil; if the mixture doesn't cover the fillets, flip the fillets halfway through marinating. Transfer the dish to the refrigerator and let the fillets rest in the oil for 30 to 45 minutes.

3 Bring your gas or charcoal grill to high heat.

4 Once the grill is ready, at about 450°F with the coals lightly covered with ash, remove the fillets from the oil and season with black pepper and sea salt. Place the fillets on the grill, skin side down, and cook for 2 to 3 minutes per side. Transfer to a large cutting board and let rest for 10 minutes. Serve warm.

TOOLS

Saucepan

INGREDIENTS

½ cup olive oil

4 garlic cloves, minced

2 tablespoons white wine vinegar

Juice from ¼ small lemon

2 teaspoons fresh rosemary

1 teaspoon fresh sage

½ teaspoon fresh thyme

8 trout fillets, about 2 pounds

Coarsely ground black pepper

Sea salt

FLOUNDER WITH BACON-WRAPPED ASPARAGUS

Makes 6 servings / Active Time: 30 minutes / Total Time: 1 hour and 15 minutes

Grilled flounder is so delicate that it breaks at the touch of a fork. Luckily, the asparagus and bacon will provide a bit of heft to this delicious, dainty dish.

1   Season the flounder fillets with black pepper and sea salt and place each fillet on a sheet of aluminum foil. Divide the clarified butter and dry white wine evenly across the fillets, and then do the same with the tomato, onions, and garlic. Top each fillet with 2 sprigs of thyme, and then fold the bottom half of the aluminum foil over the top, forming a tight crease along the sides of the fillets.

2   Preheat your gas or charcoal grill to high heat.

3   On a large cutting board, arrange the asparagus into groups of 4 or 5. Spread the bacon strips apart, and then place each asparagus spear onto the end of 1 strip of bacon. Roll the bacon strip around each asparagus spear. Once rolled tight, either pierce through the center with a long toothpick or tie with butcher's twine. Set the bundles beside the grill.

4   Once the grill is ready, at about 450°F with the coals lightly covered with ash, place the packets containing the flounder fillets on the grill, cover the grill, and cook for about 9 minutes, while flipping once. The fillets are done when their centers feel firm when poked. Transfer to a large cutting board, discard the foil packets, and let rest for 10 to 15 minutes.

5   While the flounder rests, place the asparagus on the grill and cook until the bacon and the asparagus are both charred, about 5 to 10 minutes.

6   Remove the asparagus from the grill and serve alongside the flounder fillets and lemon wedges.

TOOLS

Aluminum foil

Handful of long toothpicks, or 1 to 2 feet butcher's twine

INGREDIENTS

FOR THE FLOUNDER

4 large flounder fillets

Coarsely ground black pepper

Sea salt

4 tablespoons butter, clarified

4 teaspoons dry white wine

1 small tomato, seeded and diced

2 small white onions, minced

2 garlic cloves, sliced

8 sprigs of thyme

1 small lemon, sliced into wedges, for serving

FOR THE ASPARAGUS

1½ pounds asparagus, cut into 4-inch pieces

4 to 6 thick-cut slices of bacon

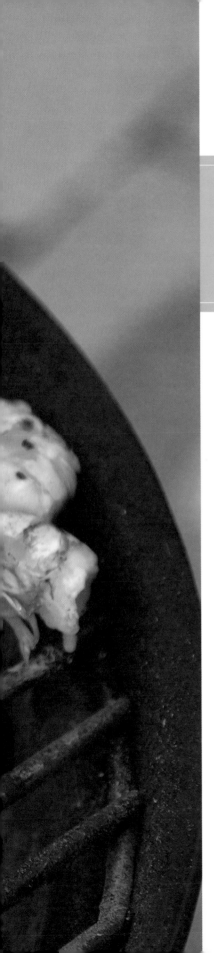

SPICY SHRIMP

Makes 4 to 6 servings / Active Time: 15 minutes / Total Time: 35 minutes

This fiery dish is one of my father's recipes and while it is not for the faint of heart, it is one of my summertime favorites.

INGREDIENTS

1 tablespoon celery salt

¼ teaspoon cayenne pepper

¼ teaspoon paprika

¼ teaspoon allspice

1 teaspoon coarsely ground black pepper

½ teaspoon kosher salt

30 large shrimp, peeled and deveined

2 tablespoons olive oil

1 Place all of the seasonings in a small bowl and stir to combine.

2 Place the shrimp in a large bowl and toss with the olive oil. Add the spicy mixture to the bowl and toss to coat evenly. Set aside while preparing the grill.

3 Preheat your gas or charcoal grill to medium-high heat.

4 Once the grill is ready, at about 425°F with the coals lightly covered with ash, place the shrimp on the grill and cook until the shrimp are slightly firm and opaque throughout. Remove from grill and let cool for 5 minutes. Serve warm.

ONION-AND-GARLIC SMOKED MUSSELS

Makes 4 to 6 servings / Active Time: 30 minutes / Total Time: 1 hour and 10 minutes

These mussels are seasoned with just enough lemon and garlic to ensure that their lightness doesn't get lost. You can also use them in the Seafood Stew in Tomato Broth (see page 358) for an added kick.

1 In a large bowl, combine the mussels, parsley, minced garlic cloves, and olive oil and toss evenly. Next, squeeze the lemon halves over the mussels and then season with black pepper and sea salt.

2 An hour before grilling, add the yellow onion and 4 remaining garlic cloves to a bowl of warm water and let soak.

3 Preheat your gas or charcoal grill to medium-high heat.

4 Once the grill is ready, at about 425°F with the coals lightly covered with ash, toss the soaked onion and garlic cloves over the coals or into the smoker box. Wait 5 minutes for the smoke to develop (there will not be as much smoke as from traditional wood chips). Place the mussels into a grill basket or on a sheet of aluminum foil and place on the grill. Cover the grill and cook for about 10 minutes, until the majority of the mussels have opened.

5 Remove the opened mussels. For any mussels that haven't opened, try cooking them a bit longer and throw them out if they don't open. Transfer the mussels to a large bowl and let rest, uncovered, for 5 to 10 minutes before serving.

TOOLS

Grill basket or aluminum foil

Smoker box (for gas grill)

INGREDIENTS

2 to 3 pounds mussels, cleaned and debearded

4 tablespoons flat-leaf parsley, chopped

8 garlic cloves; 4 minced, 4 whole

4 tablespoons olive oil

1 lemon, halved

Coarsely ground black pepper

Sea salt

1 yellow onion, quartered

STRIPED BASS WITH LEMON-HERB QUINOA

Makes 4 to 6 servings / **Active Time: 30 minutes** / **Total Time: 1 hour and 30 minutes**

The striped bass is a flavor-packed fish, so I recommend seasoning it with nothing more than a little fresh orange juice, some rosemary, salt, and pepper.

1 Squeeze the orange half over the striped bass. Next, season with the rosemary leaves, black pepper, and sea salt. Cover and let rest at room temperature for about 1 hour.

2 Preheat your gas or charcoal grill to medium-high heat.

3 Prepare the quinoa while the grill heats. Add the quinoa, olive oil, water, oregano, and rosemary to a saucepan. Set over medium heat and bring to a boil. Once boiling, reduce to a simmer and cover the saucepan with a lid for about 15 minutes, until the liquid has been absorbed and the quinoa is fluffy. Stir in parsley and lemon juice, and then season with coarsely ground black pepper and sea salt. Transfer the quinoa to a bowl, cover, and set aside.

4 Once the grill is ready, at about 425°F with the coals lightly covered with ash, place the bass on the grill for about 6 to 7 minutes, then flip over. Finish cooking the fish for another 6 to 7 minutes until the fish is juicy and opaque in the middle.

5 Remove the striped bass from the grill and transfer to a large cutting board. Cover and let rest for 5 to 10 minutes before serving. Serve warm alongside the Lemon-Herb Quinoa.

TOOLS

Saucepan

INGREDIENTS

FOR THE BASS

½ large orange

2 whole striped bass, each about 2 pounds, gutted and cleaned

Leaves from 2 sprigs of rosemary

Coarsely ground black pepper

Sea salt

FOR THE QUINOA

1 cup quinoa

1 tablespoon olive oil

2 cups water

1 teaspoon oregano, minced

1 teaspoon rosemary, minced

3 tablespoons parsley, minced

Juice from ½ lemon

Coarsely ground black pepper

Sea salt

SEAFOOD STEW IN TOMATO BROTH

Makes 4 to 6 servings / Active Time: 45 minutes / Total Time: 1 hour

Always a favorite among seafood lovers, this classic dish tastes best when served in a slightly smoky tomato broth.

TOOLS

Dutch oven

INGREDIENTS

¼ cup olive oil

1 large shallot, minced

4 garlic cloves, minced

2 slices of thick-cut bacon, chopped (optional)

¼ small green pepper, chopped

½ teaspoon dried oregano

½ teaspoon red pepper flakes

3 cups plum tomatoes, stemmed and crushed

2 tablespoons flat-leaf parsley leaves

2 thyme sprigs

1 bay leaf

Juice from ½ small lemon

2 cups clam juice

1 cup dry white wine

24 littleneck clams, scrubbed

18 mussels, scrubbed and debearded

14 large shrimp, peeled and deveined

10 (2 x 1 inch) pieces of striped bass

Coarsely ground black pepper

Sea salt

Crusty bread, for serving

1   Place a large Dutch oven on your gas or charcoal grill and bring to medium-high heat. Leave the grill covered while heating, as it will add a faint smoky flavor to the pot.

2   Once the grill is ready, at about 425°F with the coals lightly covered with ash, heat the olive oil in the Dutch oven. When the oil is hot, add the shallot and minced garlic and cook for about 2 minutes, until the shallot is translucent and the garlic is golden but not browned. Add the bacon (if using), green pepper, oregano, and red pepper flakes and cook until soft, about 5 minutes.

3   Add the tomatoes, parsley, thyme, bay leaf, lemon juice, clam juice, and dry white wine and boil until thickened, about 15 minutes. Stir in the clams, mussels, and shrimp and cook until the majority of the clams and mussels open and the shrimp is firm. Make sure to discard any mussels and clams that do not open. Add the pieces of striped bass and cook for another 3 minutes until they are opaque through the middle.

4   Remove the Dutch oven from heat, discard the bay leaf, and season with black pepper and salt. Serve in warmed bowls with crusty bread.

VEGETARIAN GRILLING

VEGETARIAN GRILLING

ONE OF MY BEST FRIENDS IS A VEGETARIAN, and when she learned that I was setting off to write a grilling book for home cooks, she said, "Wow, I wish they had vegetarian grilling recipes." She was right, vegetarians and grilling are traditionally like olive oil and water: they just don't mix. I thought back on the times we went to Hometown BBQ, an amazing barbecue joint in Brooklyn's Red Hook neighborhood, and realized that all she could really eat was the cornbread, potato salad, and pickles.

But just why is the idea of vegetarian grilling so foreign to us? Sure, there are side dishes that are vegetarian (which is what my friend orders at every barbecue restaurant we've been to), but why are there no meals? After all, vegetables have so much natural flavor! So I set off to create a handful of recipes that can initiate our vegetarian friends into the grilling world.

For vegetarian takes on a couple of old classics, check out the Black Bean Burgers (see page 366) and the Tofu Tacos with Avocado Crema (see pages 374–75). For a recipe that's sure to stand out at any barbecue, try the Goat Cheese and Pizzaiola-Stuffed Zucchini (see page 365). To ease your way in, try out any number of grilled vegetarian sides, from the Curry Asparagus over Brown Rice (see page 369) to the Mexican Street Corn (see page 377).

GOAT CHEESE AND PIZZAIOLA-STUFFED ZUCCHINI

Makes 4 to 6 servings / Active Time: 20 minutes / Total Time: 35 minutes

Zucchini can be stuffed with just about anything, but goat cheese brings a unique texture and taste to the table. The addition of the Pizzaiola Sauce makes for a perfect meal.

1 Preheat your gas or charcoal grill to high heat.

2 While waiting for your grill to heat up, slice the zucchini in half lengthwise. Using a spoon, hollow out the zucchini by removing the seeds, creating a nice trough. Season the halves with a little black pepper and sea salt. Next, evenly spread the goat cheese in the troughs of each zucchini, and then top the goat cheese with the Pizzaiola Sauce. Cover the stuffed zucchinis and place alongside your grill.

3 Once the grill is ready, at about 450°F with the coals lightly covered with ash, place the stuffed zucchinis on the grill stuffed side up and grill for about 10 to 15 minutes, until zucchini skins are charred, the cheese has melted, and the sauce is bubbling.

4 Remove from the grill and let rest for 10 minutes before serving.

VARIATION

To add a little spice to this recipe, consider adding a finely chopped jalapeño pepper after stuffing the zucchini with the goat cheese.

INGREDIENTS

4 zucchini

Coarsely ground black pepper

Sea salt

15 oz. goat cheese

2 cups Pizzaiola Sauce
(see pages 228–29)

BLACK BEAN BURGERS

Makes 6 servings / Active Time: 30 minutes / Total Time: 45 minutes

The meaty texture of the black beans and the tangy adobo sauce will have even the most fervent meat lover coming back for seconds.

1 Preheat your gas or charcoal grill to medium-low heat.

2 Add 1 can of black beans, the onion, garlic, jalapeño pepper, cumin, cilantro, chipotles, adobo sauce, and egg to a food processor and pulse until combined. Next, remove the mixture from food processor and transfer to a large bowl. Add the remaining can of black beans and the bread crumbs to the bowl and stir thoroughly. Using your hands, divide the mixture into 6 patties, each about 1 to 1½ inches thick.

3 Once the grill is ready, at about 350°F with the coals lightly covered with ash, place the patties on the grill. Season with black pepper and sea salt and grill on each side for about 6 minutes. A couple minutes before the burgers are finished, place the hamburger buns on the grill and toast for 1 or 2 minutes.

4 Remove the buns and burgers from the grill and let rest for 5 to 10 minutes before serving. Serve with your favorite toppings and condiments.

VARIATION

To make this a little healthier, substitute quinoa for the bread crumbs. Place ¼ cup of quinoa and ⅓ cup water in a saucepan and bring to a boil over high heat. Once boiling, reduce the heat and simmer for about 10 to 15 minutes until the quinoa is soft and the liquid has been absorbed.

TOOLS

Food processor

INGREDIENTS

2 (14 oz.) cans of black beans, rinsed and drained

1 yellow onion, minced

3 garlic cloves, minced

1 small jalapeño pepper

¾ teaspoon cumin

2 tablespoons fresh cilantro, minced

2 chipotles in adobo, minced

1 teaspoon adobo sauce

1 egg

¾ cup bread crumbs

Coarsely ground black pepper

Sea salt

6 hamburger buns, for serving

CURRY ASPARAGUS OVER BROWN RICE

Makes 4 to 6 servings / Active Time: 25 minutes / Total Time: 40 minutes

Asparagus is one of the best vegetables to grill. Serve it over brown rice for a vegetarian meal that has tons of fiber and protein.

1 Cook the brown rice according to the instructions on the packaging. Once cooked, transfer it to a bowl and cover with aluminum foil so that it stays warm while you grill.

2 While your rice is cooking, rinse and dry the asparagus. Place in a baking dish, add the olive oil, and toss to coat. Combine the curry powder, cumin, red pepper flakes, mint leaves, black pepper, and sea salt and add this mixture to the dish. Stir until the asparagus spears are evenly coated.

3 Preheat your gas or charcoal grill to medium heat.

4 Once the grill is ready, at about 400°F with the coals lightly covered with ash, place your seasoned asparagus on the grill and cook for about 10 minutes, turning frequently, until the asparagus is charred. Remove and serve over the rice.

INGREDIENTS

1 cup brown rice

1 bunch of asparagus

½ cup olive oil

2 teaspoons curry powder

½ teaspoon cumin

Pinch of red pepper flakes

½ cup mint leaves

Coarsely ground black pepper

Sea salt

GRILLED ZUCCHINI SANDWICHES WITH OLIVE TAPENADE

Makes 4 servings / Active Time: 15 minutes / Total Time: 30 minutes

This sandwich is perfect for those nights where you don't know what to make and want something easy and delicious. The Olive Tapenade is a nice contrast to the richness of the avocado.

1 Preheat your gas or charcoal grill to medium heat. While the grill heats, lightly brush your zucchini with olive oil.

2 Once the grill is ready, at about 400°F with the coals lightly covered with ash, place your sliced zucchini on the grill and cook for about 3 to 5 minutes, flipping over once, until the zucchini is nicely charred. Remove and set on a plate.

3 Next, brush both sides of your sourdough slices lightly with olive oil and place on the grill. Toast the sourdough for approximately 2 minutes on each side, and then remove from grill.

4 To create your sandwiches, spread the Olive Tapenade on each slice of toasted sourdough. Place the zucchini, basil leaves, mozzarella, tomatoes, and avocado on the bread and season with black pepper and sea salt. Form into sandwiches and enjoy.

NOTE: *One of the most important parts of making a good sandwich is the placement of the tomatoes, since the last thing you want is soggy bread. Always make sure your tomatoes go toward the center of the sandwich, that way, their juices don't go directly onto the bread.*

INGREDIENTS

1 zucchini, sliced into ½-inch strips

¼ cup extra virgin olive oil

1 loaf of sourdough bread, cut into ¾-inch slices

Olive Tapenade (see page 223)

20 to 30 basil leaves

¾ pound fresh mozzarella, sliced into ¼-inch strips

2 plum tomatoes, sliced into ¼-inch strips

Flesh from 1 avocado, sliced thin

Coarsely ground black pepper

Sea salt

FLATBREAD WITH ZA'ATAR

Makes 4 servings / Active Time: 15 minutes / Total Time: 20 minutes

A classic Middle Eastern dish, Flatbread with Za'atar is a perfect side. Put it on a platter along with marinated olives, hummus, and feta, and you've got a nice light meal.

INGREDIENTS

4 store-bought flatbreads

¼ cup extra virgin olive oil

2 tablespoon dried oregano

2 tablespoons fresh thyme, minced

¼ cup toasted sesame seeds (see note)

1 tablespoon lemon zest

1 Preheat your gas or charcoal grill to medium heat. While the grill heats, lightly brush your flatbreads with some of the olive oil.

2 Once the grill is ready, at about 400°F with the coals lightly covered with ash, place your flatbreads on the grill and cook for about 3 to 5 minutes per side, until each side has grill marks and is nice and toasty. Once cooked, remove the flatbreads and transfer to a cutting board.

3 In a small bowl, combine oregano, thyme, sesame seeds, and lemon zest. This is your Za'atar.

4 Brush your flatbreads with the remaining olive oil and then season with the Za'atar. Cut the flatbreads into strips and serve immediately.

NOTE: *To toast the sesame seeds, heat 1 teaspoon of olive oil in a small frying pan. Add the sesame seeds to the pan and cook for about 2 to 3 minutes until golden, being sure not to brown them. Remove and set the seeds on paper towels to drain.*

TOFU TACOS WITH AVOCADO CREMA

Makes 4 to 6 servings / Active Time: 25 minutes / Total Time: 40 minutes

Tofu is largely tasteless, making it the perfect vehicle for your favorite spices. Make sure to give the tofu as much time to marinate as you can, as it will show in the end result.

1 Preheat your gas or charcoal grill to medium heat.

2 While the grill is heating, slice your tofu into rectangular strips (about 3 inches long) and place them in a bowl. Next, add the paprika, cumin, garlic powder, lime juice, and olive oil and toss so that the tofu is evenly coated. Set aside.

3 Prepare the crema. Add the avocado, cilantro, garlic cloves, jalapeño, lime juice, and olive oil to a food processor and pulse until smooth. Season with black pepper and sea salt, remove, and set aside.

4 Once the grill is ready, at about 400°F with the coals lightly covered with ash, place the marinated tofu strips on the grill and cook for about 2 minutes per side, until grill marks appear on the tofu. Remove and set aside.

5 Place the tortillas on the grilling surface. Cook them for about 20 to 30 seconds per side, and then remove and stack them all together on one plate. Let them rest for about 10 minutes or so. It is important to stack them in one pile (imagine a stack of pancakes) since the tortillas will become too soft if they cool too much.

6 To serve, start with the tortillas at the bottom of the stack. Place the tortilla on the plate, and then add the tofu. Garnish with the onion, cilantro, tomato, and, if desired, corn. Serve with the crema on the side.

TOOLS

Food processor

INGREDIENTS

FOR THE TACOS

1 package extra-firm tofu, rinsed and drained

2 tablespoons smoked paprika

1 teaspoon ground cumin

1 teaspoon garlic powder

Juice from 1 small lime

2 tablespoons extra virgin olive oil

15 to 20 corn tortillas, homemade (pages 402–3) or store-bought

1 small red onion, chopped, for garnish

½ bunch of cilantro, chopped, for garnish

1 plum tomato, chopped, for garnish

Corn kernels, for garnish (optional)

FOR THE AVOCADO CREMA

Flesh from 2 avocados

½ bunch of cilantro, minced

2 garlic cloves, minced

1 small jalapeño pepper, seeded and minced

Juice from 1 lime

3 tablespoons extra virgin olive oil

Coarsely ground black pepper

Sea salt

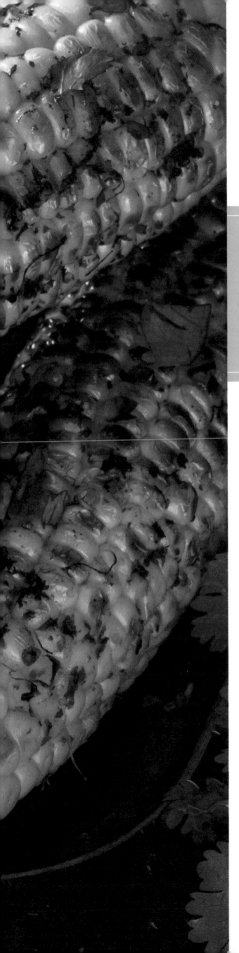

MEXICAN STREET CORN

Makes 4 servings / Active Time: 15 minutes / Total Time: 25 minutes

Cotija is a Mexican cheese that adds saltiness to the corn and balances the sweetness of the ancho chili powder. If you can't find Cotija, Parmesan is a solid substitute.

INGREDIENTS

¼ cup mayonnaise

¼ cup sour cream

¼ cup fresh cilantro, minced, plus more for garnish

½ cup Cotija or Parmesan cheese, plus more for garnish

1 garlic clove, minced

Juice from ½ small lime

½ teaspoon ancho chili powder

4 ears of corn, shucked

1　Bring your gas or charcoal grill to medium-high heat.

2　Place the mayonnaise, sour cream, cilantro, cheese, garlic, lime juice, and ancho chili powder in a small bowl and whisk until well combined.

3　Once the grill is ready, about 425°F with the coals lightly covered in ash, place the ears of corn on the grill. Cook for about 7 to 9 minutes, turning frequently, until the corn is brown and blistered.

4　When the corn is finished, remove it from the grill and place alongside the mayonnaise-and-cheese mixture. Using a brush, coat the corn evenly with the mixture. Garnish with additional cilantro and cheese and serve.

SMASHED POTATOES

Makes 4 to 6 servings / Active Time: 25 minutes / Total Time: 40 minutes

There is no greater testament to your grilling prowess like grilled potatoes, which acquire a charred sweetness that's hard to resist.

1 Add the potatoes to a medium saucepan, cover with water, and bring to a boil over medium-high heat. Once boiling, reduce to a simmer and let cook for about 18 to 23 minutes, until the potatoes can easily be pierced by a fork. Drain and then set the potatoes on a cutting board to cool.

2 Using your hands or the back of a wooden spatula, begin gently "smashing" the potatoes. You want to press them firmly so that they are smashed but still intact. Transfer to a large platter or baking sheet. Drizzle with olive oil and then sprinkle the rosemary and thyme over the potatoes. Season with black pepper and sea salt.

3 Bring your gas or charcoal grill to medium-high heat. Once the grill is ready, about 425°F with the coals lightly covered with ash, place the potatoes on the grill and cook until they are browned and crisp, about 4 to 6 minutes per side. For extra crispy potatoes, grill for 6 to 8 minutes. When finished, remove the potatoes from the grill and serve immediately.

TOOLS

Saucepan

INGREDIENTS

20 small potatoes, washed

3 tablespoons olive oil

1 tablespoon rosemary, chopped

1 tablespoon thyme, minced

Coarsely ground black pepper

Sea salt

BAKED POTATOES ON THE GRILL

Makes 4 to 6 servings / Active Time: 15 minutes / Total Time: 1 hour and 15 minutes

Nothing beats the classics. Serve these with your choice of toppings, or slather in butter for an irresistible side dish at any gathering.

TOOLS

Aluminum foil

INGREDIENTS

4 potatoes
(I prefer Idaho or russet)

3 tablespoons olive oil

Sea salt

1 Preheat your gas or charcoal grill to medium-low heat.

2 While waiting for the grill to heat up, use a fork to poke holes in the potatoes. Use a brush to coat the potatoes with olive oil and then season with sea salt. Wrap each potato in aluminum foil and set them alongside the grill.

3 Once the grill is ready, about 325°F to 350°F with the coals lightly covered in ash, place the foil-wrapped potatoes directly on the grill. Cover the grill and cook for about 1 hour, turning the potatoes just once or twice while grilling. To test for doneness, open the aluminum foil covering one potato and poke with a fork; it should easily pierce the potato.

4 Remove from the grill and serve.

CHARRED SWEET POTATOES

Makes 4 servings / Active Time: 45 minutes / Total Time: 1 hour

Though most often baked, sweet potatoes taste even sweeter when grilled. Consider throwing soaked maple wood chips on the fire and grilling with the lid closed for additional flavor.

INGREDIENTS

4 large sweet potatoes

2 tablespoons olive oil

Coarsely ground black pepper

Sea salt

1 Rub the sweet potatoes with olive oil and then season with black pepper and sea salt.

2 Bring your gas or charcoal grill to medium-high heat.

3 Once the grill is ready, about 425°F with the coals lightly covered with ash, place the sweet potatoes on the grill and cook for 45 minutes, turning every 15 minutes or so until finished. When done, a fork should easily pierce the sweet potatoes.

4 Remove from the grill and serve.

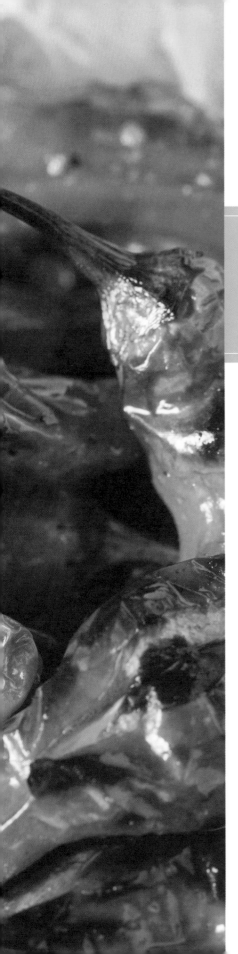

SHISHITO PEPPERS

Makes 4 servings / Active Time: 10 minutes / Total Time: 30 minutes

These peppers are best when charred and blistered, as grilling draws out their natural sweetness.

TOOLS

Cast-iron skillet

INGREDIENTS

2 to 3 cups whole shishito peppers

2 tablespoons olive oil

Coarsely ground black pepper

Sea salt

1   In a cast-iron skillet, combine the shishito peppers and olive oil, and then season with black pepper and sea salt.

2   Bring your gas or charcoal grill to medium-high heat.

3   Once the grill is ready, about 425°F with the coals lightly covered in ash, place the cast-iron skillet on the grill and cook the peppers until blistered, about 8 to 10 minutes.

4   Remove from grill and serve immediately.

CUBANELLE PEPPERS AND PLUM TOMATOES

Makes 4 servings / Active Time: 10 minutes / Total Time: 30 minutes

This mix of spicy cubanelle peppers and hot, juicy tomatoes creates a truly memorable side dish.

INGREDIENTS

6 cubanelle peppers

3 plum tomatoes, halved

2 tablespoons olive oil

Coarsely ground black pepper

Sea salt

Leaves from 1 sprig of rosemary, for garnish (optional)

1 In a large bowl, combine the cubanelle peppers, plum tomatoes, and olive oil and mix thoroughly. Season with black pepper and sea salt and set aside.

2 Preheat your gas or charcoal grill to medium-high heat.

3 Once the grill is ready, about 425°F with the coals lightly covered with ash, place the peppers and tomatoes on the grill and cook until charred, about 5 to 10 minutes.

4 Remove from grill, garnish with rosemary, if desired, and serve warm.

CHARRED SCALLIONS

Makes 4 to 6 servings / Active Time: 10 minutes / Total Time: 20 minutes

A quick dish that never fails to liven up a meal. This is a perfect side for the Black Bean Burgers (see page 366), as well as any of the steak and poultry dishes.

TOOLS

Cast-iron skillet

INGREDIENTS

2 bunches of scallions
(about 15 to 20)

Juice from ½ small lemon or lime

1 tablespoon olive oil

Coarsely ground black pepper

Sea salt

1   Combine the scallions, lemon or lime juice, and olive oil in a cast-iron skillet. Season with pepper and salt and set aside.

2   Bring your gas or charcoal grill to medium-high heat.

3   Once the grill is ready, about 425°F with the coals lightly covered with ash, place the cast-iron skillet on the grill and cook the scallions until tender and charred, about 5 minutes.

4   Remove from heat and serve warm.

BALSAMIC PEPPERS

Makes 4 to 6 servings / Active Time: 15 minutes / Total Time: 30 minutes

The sweet and tart nature of this dish is perfect company for a number of meals, but it pairs particularly well with marinated tofu.

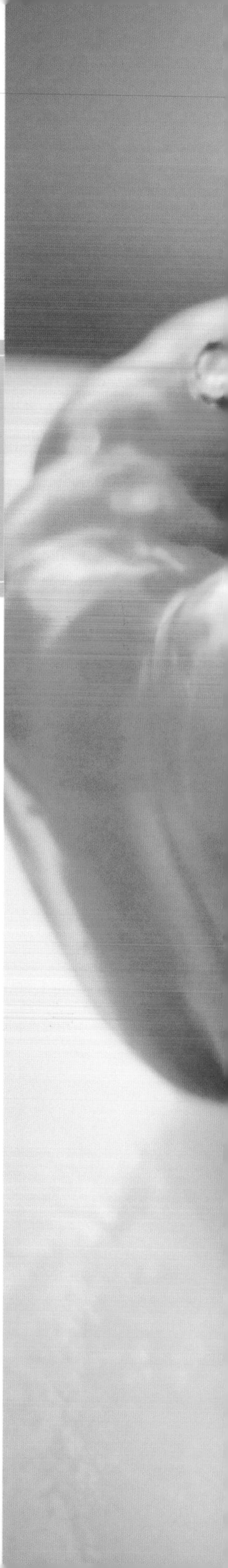

TOOLS

Cast-iron skillet

INGREDIENTS

2 red bell peppers, stemmed, seeded, and quartered

2 yellow bell peppers, stemmed, seeded, and quartered

2 green bell peppers, stemmed, seeded, and quartered

4 tablespoons olive oil

2 tablespoons balsamic vinegar

8 basil leaves

Coarsely ground black pepper

Sea salt

1 pound arugula, for serving

1 Place all of the ingredients, except for the arugula, in a large bowl and combine.

2 Place a cast-iron skillet on your gas or charcoal grill and bring the grill to medium heat. Leave the grill covered while heating, as it will add a faint smoky flavor to the skillet.

3 Once the grill is ready, about 400°F with the coals lightly covered with ash, place the peppers in the skillet and cook until tender and lightly charred, about 7 to 9 minutes.

4 Remove from grill and serve over arugula.

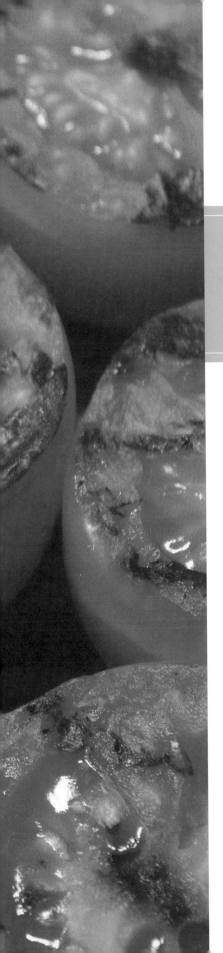

TOMATOES WITH GARLIC

Makes 4 to 6 servings / Active Time: 15 minutes / Total Time: 35 minutes

Nothing says summer like this side dish. Garlic and tomato is an age-old pairing that really shines when cooked on the grill.

INGREDIENTS

10 tomatoes

4 large garlic cloves, chopped

¼ cup olive oil

4 chives, minced

Coarsely ground black pepper

Sea salt

1   Bring your gas or charcoal grill to medium-high heat.

2   Stem the tomatoes, cut them in half, and put them in a medium bowl.

3   Add the garlic, olive oil, and chives, and then season with black pepper and sea salt. Set aside.

4   Once the grill is ready, at about 425°F with the coals lightly covered with ash, place the tomatoes on the grill and cook until their skins are charred, about 5 minutes. Serve warm.

CHARRED SUMMER SQUASH

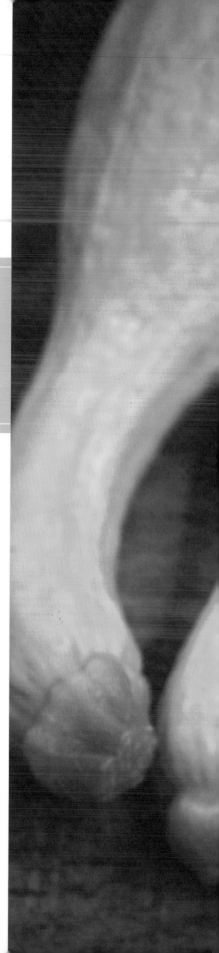

Makes 4 to 6 servings / Active Time: 10 minutes / Total Time: 20 minutes

Here's the perfect side to add a splash of color to any meal. Whip this up when you need a light, lovely side and don't have much time.

INGREDIENTS

1 medium yellow squash

¼ cup olive oil

Coarsely ground black pepper

Sea salt

1 Bring your gas or charcoal grill to medium-high heat.

2 While waiting, cut the squash diagonally into long slices. Add the squash to a small bowl and combine with the olive oil, black pepper, and sea salt.

3 Once the grill is ready, about 425°F with the coals lightly covered with ash, place the squash slices on the grill and cook, while flipping once, until tender—about 10 minutes.

4 Remove from grill and serve warm.

ZUCCHINI WITH SEA SALT

Makes 4 to 6 servings / Active Time: 15 minutes / Total Time: 35 minutes

When seasoned generously with lemon juice and some black pepper and sea salt, this simple grilled zucchini is sure to stand out at your next get-together.

INGREDIENTS

4 zucchini, halved lengthwise

Juice from ¼ small lemon

Coarsely ground black pepper

Sea salt

1 Bring your gas or charcoal grill to medium-high heat.

2 While waiting, toss the zucchini, lemon juice, black pepper, and salt together in a small bowl and set aside.

3 Once the grill is ready, about 425°F with the coals lightly covered with ash, add the zucchini to the grill and cook until charred, about 10 to 15 minutes.

4 Remove from the grill and serve warm.

CAJUN OKRA

Makes 4 servings / Active Time: 10 minutes / Total Time: 15 minutes

A favorite in the South, okra possesses countless health benefits. Luckily, it's also delicious.

TOOLS

10 bamboo skewers, soaked in water prior to grilling

INGREDIENTS

1 pound fresh okra

¼ cup butter, melted

¼ cup Cajun Rub (see page 94)

Coarsely ground black pepper

Sea salt

1   Preheat your gas or charcoal grill to medium-high.

2   Lay 5 or 6 pieces of okra side by side. Take a wet bamboo skewer and run it all the way through the okra. Brush the skewered okra with melted butter to coat and then season with the rub, pepper, and salt. Repeat until all of the okra have been skewered.

3   When your grill is ready, about 425°F with the coals lightly covered in ash, place the skewers on the grill about 1 inch apart. Grill on each side for about 3 to 4 minutes, or until the okra is charred. Remove from the grill and serve immediately.

EGGPLANT WITH HERBS

Makes 4 to 6 servings / Active Time: 30 minutes / Total Time: 45 minutes

This Italian-inspired dish can either stand on its own or be used as a side. Be warned, though, it tends to overshadow anything else on the table.

INGREDIENTS

½ small white onion, minced

½ cup olive oil

¼ cup parsley leaves, chopped

1 medium eggplant, halved lengthwise

Coarsely ground black pepper

Sea salt

1 Place the onion, olive oil, and parsley in a roasting pan and stir until thoroughly combined. Add the eggplant halves, stir to coat, and let stand at room temperature while you prepare the grill.

2 Bring your gas or charcoal grill to medium-high heat. Designate two sections of the grill, one for direct heat and the other for indirect heat. To do so, simply pile the coals on one side of a charcoal grill or turn off one of the burners on a gas grill.

3 Once the grill is ready, about 425°F, remove the eggplant halves from the roasting pan and place them over indirect heat. Season with black pepper and sea salt, cover the grill, and cook for about 15 to 25 minutes, until the eggplant has softened.

4 Remove from grill and serve warm.

CORN TORTILLAS

Makes 15 to 20 tortillas / Active Time: 30 minutes / Total Time: 1 hour and 30 minutes

For an authentic tortilla, use a tortilla press. While it is possible to make tortillas without a press, it can be challenging. This recipe becomes easier the more you make it, so appoint one day a week as taco time and get to work. To serve this recipe, take any meat listed in this book and slice it to fit the tortilla, or make the Tofu Tacos with Avocado Crema (see pages 374–75).

1 Using your hands, combine the masa harina, hot water, and salt in a large bowl and work until the mixture forms a dough. This will take about 4 to 5 minutes of constant mixing. If the mixture is too dry, add 1-teaspoon increments of hot water until you reach the desired consistency. Form the dough into one large ball and place in the center of the bowl. Cover with a cloth towel and let the dough rest for about 1 hour.

2 While the dough rests, prepare the resealable bag. Take a pair of scissors and cut down the left and right seams of the bag. You want the bag to be able to open like a V since you will use it to prevent the tortillas from sticking to the tortilla press. Take the bag and lay it flat across the tortilla press to form a protective layer.

3 When the tortilla dough has rested for 1 hour, reshape the ball of dough with your hands. Next, take small, meatball-sized clumps of the dough and place them in the center of the tortilla press. Close, press down firmly, and remove the thin tortilla. Do this until all of the dough is used up.

4 Preheat a cast-iron skillet on a grill set to medium heat. Once hot, add the tortillas one at a time and cook for about 1 minute per side, until the center of the tortilla begins to rise. This can take some practice to notice. Flip and cook for another minute. Brown marks should be speckled across both sides of the tortilla, but it should not look burnt.

5 Stack the tortillas on paper towels and let rest. It is important to stack the tortillas in a pile since it will help them accumulate moisture and keep them flexible.

NOTE: *Instead of a tortilla press, you can also use two large, heavy cookbooks. Simply place one cookbook on the table and top with parchment or wax paper. Next, set the ball of dough on top of the parchment paper. Finally, place another piece of parchment paper over the dough, and then press down with a second cookbook so that a tortilla is formed. It should be about ⅛-inch thick.*

TOOLS

1 large resealable plastic bag or
2 pieces of parchment paper

1 tortilla press or 2 heavy cookbooks

Cast-iron skillet

INGREDIENTS

2 cups masa harina

1½ cups warm water (100°F), plus more
as needed

1 teaspoon kosher salt

ARTICHOKES WITH GARLIC

Makes 4 to 5 servings / Active Time: 25 minutes / Total Time: 45 minutes

Artichokes need to be softened up in boiling water before cooking, but their mild, slightly nutty taste makes them ideal for the grill.

1 Fill a stockpot with water. Add the lemon juice and bring to boil over medium-high heat.

2 Bring your gas or charcoal grill to medium-high heat.

3 When the lemon water is boiling, add the artichokes and boil until tender, about 15 minutes. Drain, transfer to a small bowl, and add the garlic, olive oil, black pepper, and sea salt. Toss to coat.

4 Once the grill is ready, about 425°F with the coals lightly covered with ash, place the artichokes on the grill and cook until lightly charred, about 6 minutes.

5 Remove from grill and serve warm.

VARIATION

To make these Cajun Artichokes, remove the lemon juice and garlic from the recipe, and only include 2 tablespoons of olive oil. Toss the artichokes, 2 tablespoons of olive oil, and 3 tablespoons of Cajun Rub (see page 94) in a bowl and then cook the artichokes on the grill for about 6 minutes.

TOOLS

Stockpot

INGREDIENTS

Juice from ½ large lemon

3 large artichokes, trimmed and halved lengthwise

5 large garlic cloves, minced

½ cup olive oil

Coarsely ground black pepper

Sea salt

PINEAPPLE SALSA

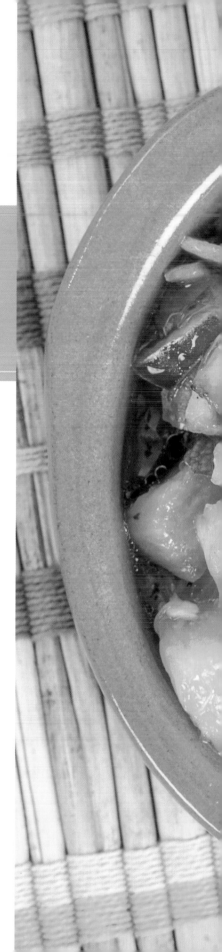

Makes 4 servings / **Active Time: 15 minutes** / **Total Time: 30 minutes**

Grilling really brings out the best in the pineapple, pepper, and onion in this tasty salsa. Serve it alongside seafood or chicken, or with the Tofu Tacos with Avocado Crema (see pages 374–75).

INGREDIENTS

1 large pineapple, peeled, cored, and cut into chunks

1 red bell pepper, peeled and cut into long strips

½ small red onion, quartered

¼ cup fresh cilantro, minced

Juice from ¼ small lime

Coarsely ground black pepper

Sea salt

1   Bring your gas or charcoal grill to medium-high heat.

2   Once the grill is ready, about 425°F with the coals lightly covered with ash, place the pineapple slices, pepper, and onion on the grill. Cook the pineapple slices until slightly browned, about 4 minutes. Remove the pineapple and set on a cutting board. Continue to grill the peppers and onion until charred, about 4 more minutes, and then remove and place on the cutting board.

3   Chop the pineapple, pepper, and onion into ½-inch cubes and transfer to a medium bowl.

4   Stir in the cilantro and lime juice and season with black pepper and sea salt. Serve chilled.

BROCCOLI WITH LIME BUTTER

Makes 4 servings / Active Time: 15 minutes / Total Time: 35 minutes

Lime and broccoli is an overlooked combination that deserves some time in the spotlight.

TOOLS

Saucepan

INGREDIENTS

6 tablespoons butter, clarified

Juice from ¼ small lime

2 garlic cloves, minced

½ teaspoon cilantro, minced

Coarsely ground black pepper

Sea salt

4 heads of broccoli, stemmed and chopped

2 tablespoons olive oil

1 Bring your gas or charcoal grill to medium heat.

2 Place the clarified butter, lime juice, garlic, and cilantro in a small saucepan and cook over very low heat while stirring occasionally. Season with black pepper and sea salt as the mixture cooks.

3 Once the grill is ready, about 400°F with the coals lightly covered with ash, brush the broccoli florets with olive oil and place them on the grill. Cook until lightly charred, about 10 minutes, and then transfer to a medium bowl.

4 Remove the Lime Butter from the stove, add to the bowl containing the broccoli, and toss to coat. Serve warm.

BRUSSELS SPROUTS

Makes 4 servings / Active Time: 10 minutes / Total Time: 30 minutes

Crispy on the outside and succulent on the inside, this flavorful side will go well with practically every dish.

TOOLS

Skewers

INGREDIENTS

2 cups Brussels sprouts, halved

3 tablespoons olive oil

1 garlic clove, minced

Coarsely ground black pepper

Sea salt

1   Bring your gas or charcoal grill to medium heat.

2   Place the Brussels sprouts, olive oil, garlic, pepper, and salt in a large bowl and stir to combine. Place 3 to 4 Brussels sprouts on each skewer and set the finished skewers on a plate beside the grill.

3   Once the grill is ready, about 400°F with the coals lightly covered with ash, place the Brussels sprouts onto the grill, cover the grill, and cook for about 5 minutes. Turn the sprouts over and cook for a few more minutes, until slightly charred all over.

4   Remove from grill and serve warm.

BROCCOLINI WITH LEMON, GARLIC, AND RED PEPPER FLAKES

Makes 4 servings / Active Time: 20 minutes / Total Time: 30 minutes

Broccolini is mild, tender, and cooks quicker than its distant cousin, broccoli. The garlic and red pepper flakes give this dish a powerful punch that will work in any season.

1 Preheat your gas or charcoal grill to medium heat.

2 While your grill heats, place the olive oil, garlic, red pepper flakes, lemon juice, and Parmesan cheese in a large bowl. Whisk to thoroughly combine. Add the broccolini to the bowl, toss to coat, and place beside the grill.

3 Once the grill is ready, at about 400°F with the coals lightly covered with ash, place the broccolini directly on the grill. Keep a close eye on the broccolini and cook for about 5 to 6 minutes per side until browned. You can also cook the broccolini on a baking sheet if you would like; simply place the broccolini on the baking sheet, place the baking sheet on the grill, cover, and cook for about 15 minutes.

4 Remove the broccolini from the grill and serve.

VARIATION

Yes, this is the vegetarian chapter. But I'd regret not mentioning that bacon makes for a lovely addition to this dish. To do this, take 4 to 6 slices of bacon, cut them into ¼-inch pieces, and then add to the bowl with the other ingredients. Make sure to cook the broccolini and bacon on a baking sheet to ensure the bacon gets the proper level of crispiness and to prevent pieces from falling through the grill grate.

TOOLS

Baking sheet (optional)

INGREDIENTS

2 tablespoons olive oil

4 garlic cloves, finely chopped

2 teaspoons red pepper flakes

Juice from 1 lemon

3 tablespoons Parmesan cheese, grated

3 to 4 heads of broccolini, trimmed and cut into florets

BEETS WITH WALNUTS

Makes 4 servings / Active Time: 20 minutes / Total Time: 1 hour

This is my mother's favorite side dish. The beets are so rich that you don't need many to satisfy everyone at the table. Make sure to prepare these on a stainless steel surface, as they will turn your wooden cutting board a startling shade of magenta that is tough to get rid of.

1 Combine the beets, walnuts, and olive oil in a large bowl and let rest for 30 minutes.

2 Place a cast-iron skillet on your gas or charcoal grill and preheat the grill to medium-high heat. Leave the grill covered while heating, as it will add a faint smoky flavor to the skillet.

3 Once the grill is ready, about 425°F with the coals lightly covered with ash, place the beets directly on the grill. Grill the beets for about 10 minutes, until tender and marked with grill lines. Transfer the beets to a large bowl and cover with aluminum foil.

4 Place the walnuts and oil in the cast-iron skillet and cook until browned, about 2 minutes. Remove and combine with the beets. Season with black pepper and sea salt and serve warm.

TOOLS

Cast-iron skillet

INGREDIENTS

6 medium beets, peeled and halved

½ cup walnuts

¼ cup olive oil

Coarsely ground black pepper

Sea salt

CAJUN GREEN BEANS

Makes 4 servings / **Active Time: 5 minutes** / **Total Time: 20 minutes**

Using the Cajun Rub turns simple green beans into a spicy snack that will have your friends and family clamoring for more—so don't hesitate to cook a double batch.

TOOLS

Cast-iron skillet

INGREDIENTS

1 pound green beans, trimmed

1 tablespoon butter, melted

2 tablespoons Cajun Rub (see page 94)

1   Place a cast-iron skillet on your gas or charcoal grill and preheat the grill to medium-high heat. Leave the grill covered while heating, as it will add a faint smoky flavor to the skillet.

2   In a small bowl, toss the green beans with the melted butter in a bowl. Add the Cajun Rub to the bowl and stir until the green beans are coated evenly.

3   Once the grill is ready, about 425°F with the coals lightly covered with ash, transfer the green beans into the cast-iron skillet. Let them cook for about 4 minutes, stirring every so often, until they are blistered and browned.

4   Transfer the green beans to a bowl and serve.

CHARRED LOTUS ROOT

Makes 4 servings / Active Time: 15 minutes / Total Time: 30 minutes

Lotus root is relatively hard to come by in the United States. Its texture is somewhere between a potato and a carrot, with holes spread across its surface. A well-cooked lotus root is crispy and extremely delicious, especially when charred on the grill. If you're intrigued, swing by your local Asian market.

1   Preheat your gas or charcoal grill to medium-low heat.

2   In a large bowl combine your lotus root slices, olive oil, and sesame oil. Season with black pepper and sea salt.

3   Once your grill is ready, about 325°F with the coals lightly covered with ash, place your lotus root slices directly on the grill. Cook for about 8 minutes per side and remove from the grill when they are crispy and brown. Serve immediately.

VARIATION

To add some classic Chinese BBQ spice to the mix, consider adding a rub to the bowl after tossing the lotus roots with olive oil and sesame oil. The rub should consist of 3 teaspoons cayenne pepper, 2 teaspoons Chinese Five-Spice Rub (see page 121), and 1 teaspoon garlic powder.

INGREDIENTS

2 large lotus roots, sliced

2 tablespoons olive oil

½ tablespoon sesame oil

Coarsely ground black pepper

Sea salt

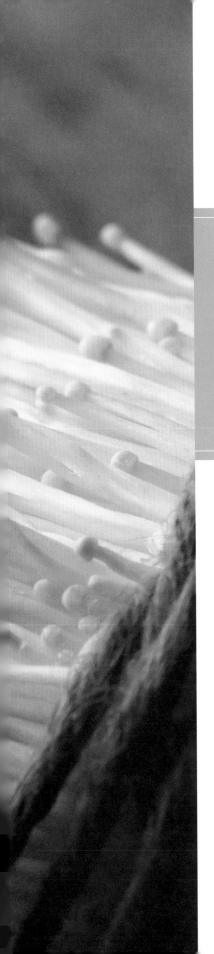

BUTTERY ENOKI MUSHROOMS

Makes 4 servings   /   Active Time: 10 minutes   /   Total Time: 20 minutes

A Chinese BBQ usually starts up around 10:00 in the evening and will run until the early hours of the morning. While many of the ingredients are familiar to those in the United States, there are a handful of foods unique to China. One vegetable that is found everywhere in Chongqing (a provincial city in the middle of China) are enoki mushrooms, which the locals refer to as "see you tomorrow mushrooms." Here they are reimagined for the grill.

1 Preheat your grill to high heat.

2 Stack 2 sheets of aluminum foil on top of each other on a cutting board. Place the mushrooms and butter in the center of the foil and top with the lemon juice. Add a pinch of black pepper and sea salt and then fold the edges of the foil upward to form a bowl. This is important since you want the mushrooms to cook in the melted butter on the grill. Close the foil over the mushrooms.

3 Once the grill is ready, about 450°F with the coals lightly covered with ash, place the mushroom packet on the grill and cook, covered, for about 12 to 15 minutes. The mushrooms should be easily pierced with a fork when finished.

4 Remove the packet from the grill, place it on a platter, and serve.

TOOLS
Aluminum foil

INGREDIENTS
4 bunches of enoki mushrooms

2 tablespoons butter

Juice of ¼ small lemon

Coarsely ground black pepper

Sea salt

DESSERTS

DESSERTS

GROWING UP, my mother always maintained a beautiful garden in our backyard. My brothers and I helped her build and install the wooden beds where she would grow all kinds of fruits and vegetables for three-quarters of the year. Neighbors would swing by our home and admire her garden, commenting on how blue her blueberries were, admiring the size of the strawberries, and asking if they would be able to have a few raspberries before they left. While my mother was always generous in sharing the bounty of her garden, deep down I was upset that I would not be able to enjoy what she gave away in a dessert.

When I think of classic summer cookout desserts, I always fall back on three fruity desserts: tarts, pies, and crisps. Not only are these desserts even more amazing when they utilize homegrown or locally grown fruits, but they are so easy to make, especially once you learn the structure of the desserts. For a tart, pie, and a crisp, the two main parts are the dough and the filling; once you perfect the dough, the filling is a breeze.

TOOLS

9-inch tart pan with
removable bottom

INGREDIENTS

FOR THE DOUGH

1 cup all-purpose flour

2 tablespoons sugar

9 tablespoons butter, chilled
and cut into pieces

3 tablespoons ice-cold water

FOR THE BLUEBERRY FILLING

4 cups fresh blueberries

⅔ cup sugar

2 tablespoons all-purpose flour

1 tablespoon lemon juice

½ teaspoon ground cinnamon

¼ teaspoon ground nutmeg

FOR THE COFFEE WHIPPED CREAM

2 cups heavy cream

½ cup sugar

¾ teaspoon finely ground
coffee

BLUEBERRY TART WITH COFFEE WHIPPED CREAM

Makes 4 to 6 servings / Active Time: 30 minutes / Total Time: 1 hour and 15 minutes

Blueberries are such a sugary fruit that they caramelize when baked and add a lovely element to any dessert. With this blueberry tart, it is important to divide the blueberries, as some will be used for the smashed filling, while the rest will be used for a beautiful topping.

1   Prepare the dough. Combine the flour and sugar by hand or with an electric mixer. Gradually add 8 tablespoons of the butter to the bowl and mix until the dough is crumbly. Stir in the water and then set your dough aside. Grease the bottom of the tart pan with the remaining butter. Place the dough in the tart pan and spread evenly across the bottom. Transfer the tart pan to the freezer and let rest for 15 to 20 minutes until firm.

2   Preheat your oven to 375°F. While waiting on your oven, prepare the blueberry filling. Place 2½ cups of the blueberries in a bowl and smash with the back of a fork. Next, whisk in the sugar, flour, lemon juice, cinnamon, and nutmeg. Remove the tart pan from the freezer and pour the mixture evenly over the dough.

3   When the oven is ready, transfer the tart pan to the oven and bake for approximately 1 hour. When the blueberries are bubbling in the pan, remove the pan from the oven. Top with the remaining blueberries and let rest for 10 minutes before serving.

4   While the blueberry tart is baking, place a bowl in the freezer and chill for 15 minutes. Once chilled, place the whipped cream ingredients into the chilled bowl and beat until stiff peaks form in the cream. Place a dollop of whipped cream on top of each piece of the blueberry tart and serve.

MIXED BERRY PIE

Makes 6 servings / Active Time: 1 hour and 15 minutes / Total Time: 2 hours and 5 minutes

This pie is perfect for the height of berry season. This recipe works well with any kind of berry, just make sure that the berries total about 7 to 8 cups.

1 Prepare the dough. Place the flour, sugar, and salt in a food processor and pulse a few times until combined. Add the pieces of butter to the processor and pulse until the mixture is crumbly, with the crumbs about the size of a pea. Finally, add the water and pulse until a smooth dough has formed. If the dough is still too thick, add water in 1-tablespoon increments.

2 Remove the dough from the food processor and, using your hands, shape into one big ball. Split the ball of dough in half and form into two separate balls. Flatten each so that the dough forms two discs. Cover each disc with plastic wrap and transfer them to the refrigerator. Let sit in the refrigerator for at least 1 hour before using.

3 Preheat your oven to 400°F. While the oven warms up, remove your dough from the refrigerator. Place one disc of dough in the greased pie plate. In a medium bowl, combine the filling ingredients and mix thoroughly. Add the mixture to the dough-lined pie plate. Take the other disc of dough and cover the berry pie, discarding any dough that hangs over the edges. Fold the dough at the edges and use a fork to pierce holes in the top of the pie.

4 When the oven is ready, transfer the pie to the oven and bake for about 45 to 55 minutes, until the dough is light brown and the filling is bubbling. Remove from oven and let rest for 10 minutes before serving.

TOOLS

Food processor

9-inch pie plate

INGREDIENTS

FOR THE DOUGH

2½ cups all-purpose flour

1 tablespoon sugar

1 teaspoon kosher salt

2 sticks of unsalted butter, cut into ½-inch pieces

6 tablespoons ice-cold water, plus more as needed

FOR THE FILLING

2 cups fresh raspberries

2 cups fresh blueberries

2 cups fresh blackberries

1 cup strawberries, halved

¼ cup all-purpose flour

½ cup sugar

½ teaspoon ground cinnamon

3 teaspoons lemon juice

APPLE PIE

Makes 6 servings / Active Time: 1 hour and 15 minutes / Total Time: 2 hours and 5 minutes

This American classic provides the perfect landing after an evening filled with grilled dishes.

1 Prepare the dough. Place the flour, sugar, and salt in a food processor and pulse a few times until combined. Add the pieces of butter to the processor and pulse until the mixture is crumbly, with the crumbs about the size of a pea. Finally, add the water and pulse until a smooth dough has formed. If the dough is still too thick, add water in 1-tablespoon increments.

2 Remove the dough from the food processor and, using your hands, shape into one big ball. Split the ball of dough in half and form into two separate balls. Flatten each so that the dough forms two discs. Cover each disc with plastic wrap and transfer them to the refrigerator. Let sit in the refrigerator for at least 1 hour before using.

3 Preheat your oven to 400°F. While the oven warms up, remove your dough from the refrigerator. Place one disc of dough in a greased pie plate. In a medium bowl, combine the filling ingredients and mix thoroughly. Add the mixture to the dough-lined pie plate. Take the other disc of dough and cover the pie, discarding any dough that hangs over the edges. Fold the dough at the edges and use a fork to pierce holes in the top of the pie.

4 When the oven is ready, transfer the pie to the oven and bake for about 45 to 55 minutes, until the dough is light brown and the filling is bubbling. Remove from oven and let rest for 10 minutes before serving.

TOOLS

Food processor

9-inch pie plate

INGREDIENTS

FOR THE DOUGH

2½ cups all-purpose flour

1 tablespoon sugar

1 teaspoon kosher salt

2 sticks of unsalted butter, cut into ½-inch pieces

6 tablespoons ice-cold water, plus more as needed

FOR THE FILLING

6 Granny Smith apples, peeled, cored, and cut into wedges

⅔ cup sugar

2 tablespoons all-purpose flour

1 teaspoon cinnamon

¼ teaspoon ground nutmeg

1 teaspoon fresh lemon juice

1 teaspoon lemon zest

1½ tablespoons unsalted butter, chilled

PEACH CRISP

Makes 6 servings / Active Time: 45 minutes / Total Time: 55 minutes

The sugary topping caramelizes in the oven to create a buttery, fruity desert that's second to none.

1 Combine the peach slices and the sugar in a medium bowl and let sit for 20 minutes.

2 Place the ½ cup of flour, oats, brown sugar, baking powder, cinnamon, and nutmeg in a mixing bowl and combine. Gradually add the butter until the mixture is crumbly. Transfer the mixing bowl to the refrigerator and let sit.

3 Preheat your oven to 375°F. Remove the peaches from the bowl, discard the juice, and combine with the remaining flour, the lemon juice, vanilla, and lemon zest. Pour the mixture into a greased baking dish, and then top with the crumbly mixture. Transfer the baking dish to the oven and cook for about 35 minutes, or until the crisp is golden brown. Remove and serve with vanilla ice cream.

TOOLS

Baking dish

INGREDIENTS

6 to 8 peaches, peeled, cored, and sliced

¼ cup granulated sugar

½ cup plus 2 tablespoons all-purpose flour

1 cup rolled oats

½ cup brown sugar

½ teaspoon baking powder

½ teaspoon ground cinnamon

¼ teaspoon ground nutmeg

2 teaspoons lemon juice

½ teaspoon vanilla extract

1 teaspoon lemon zest

1 stick of butter, chilled and cut into small pieces

Vanilla ice cream, for serving

BERRY PARFAIT WITH COCONUT CREAM

Makes 4 to 6 servings / Active Time: 10 minutes / Total Time: 15 minutes

The Coconut Cream takes this deceptively simple fruit salad to the next level, while the mashed raspberries make for a rich, colorful presentation.

1 Prepare the Coconut Cream. Remove the can of coconut milk from the refrigerator, hold it upside down for 30 seconds, and open it. The liquid should be at the top, having separated from the heavier cream.

2 Pour the liquid out of the can and reserve it for another preparation.

3 Scoop the remaining cream into a bowl and beat it with a whisk until it forms stiff peaks. Whisk in the honey or maple syrup and the vanilla component and beat until you reach your desired thickness. Place the bowl in the refrigerator.

4 Prepare the Berry Parfait. Rinse the berries and pat them dry. Scoop half of the Coconut Cream into a bowl, add ½ cup of the raspberries, and mash until fully combined. In a separate bowl, combine the remaining fruit.

5 In individual cups or jars, layer the ingredients as follows: a layer of plain Coconut Cream at the base, followed by a layer of fruit and granola (if using), a layer of the raspberry cream, and then top with more fruit and granola.

INGREDIENTS

FOR THE COCONUT CREAM

1 (13.5 oz.) can of organic coconut milk, refrigerated overnight

2 teaspoons raw honey or pure maple syrup

1 teaspoon pure vanilla extract or 1 vanilla bean, halved

FOR THE BERRY PARFAIT

1½ cups raspberries

1 cup blueberries

1 cup strawberries, sliced

Granola (optional)

BERRY DELICIOUS POPSICLES

Makes about 10 to 12 popsicles / Active Time: 10 minutes / Total Time: 3 to 5 hours

While your steaks are marinating, assemble these fresh fruit popsicles. No baking, simmering, or grilling required—just assemble the ingredients, pop them into your freezer, and enjoy the results. As you'll see from the variation below, the possibilities are endless.

1 Wash your berries and place them in your blender with the lemon juice and honey. Puree until smooth, about 30 seconds.

2 Pour the mixture into popsicle molds and insert popsicle sticks into each.

3 Freeze until popsicles hold firm, about 3 to 5 hours.

4 Briefly submerge the mold in lukewarm water. When the popsicles begin to separate from the molds, remove immediately and enjoy.

VARIATIONS

Try using kiwi slices, pineapple, or other tropical fruit combinations for an entirely different experience. Or enhance the flavor by adding fresh grated ginger, organic dark cocoa powder, pure vanilla or almond extract, unsweetened coconut flakes, or even sea salt.

TOOLS

Blender

Popsicle molds

Popsicle sticks

INGREDIENTS

3 cups berries of your choice

¼ cup lemon juice

¼ cup raw honey

STRAWBERRY SHORTCAKES WITH VANILLA WHIPPED CREAM

Makes 4 servings / Active Time: 30 minutes / Total Time: 1 hour and 15 minutes

Juicy strawberries, buttery shortbread, and homemade whipped cream form a trio that is certain to stand the test of time.

1 Preheat your oven to 400°F. Combine the strawberries and the ¼ cup of sugar in one large bowl and cover with plastic wrap. Let sit for at least 40 minutes so that the strawberries become juicy. Place the remaining sugar, flour, baking powder, lemon zest, and ground cinnamon in a mixing bowl and beat until combined. Add the heavy cream very slowly and beat until a nice doughy mixture has formed. Set aside.

2 When the oven is ready, add the doughy mixture to a greased baking dish and let it settle evenly. Transfer the dish to the oven and bake until golden, about 20 minutes. Remove the shortcake from the oven and cut into 8 pieces. Using a spatula, remove the shortcake pieces from the dish and let cool on a large plate.

3 Prepare the whipped cream. Place a bowl in the freezer and let chill for 15 minutes. Once chilled, place all of the ingredients into the bowl and beat for 5 to 10 minutes, until stiff peaks form.

4 To serve, place the whipped cream on top of a piece of shortcake, followed by a few scoops of the strawberries and their juices. Top with another piece of shortcake and serve.

TOOLS

Baking dish

INGREDIENTS

FOR THE STRAWBERRY SHORTCAKES

2 pounds strawberries, stemmed and halved

¼ cup plus 2 tablespoons sugar

2 cups all-purpose flour

2 teaspoons baking powder

½ teaspoon lemon zest

¼ teaspoon ground cinnamon

1½ cups heavy cream

FOR THE VANILLA WHIPPED CREAM

2 cups heavy cream

½ cup sugar

1 teaspoon vanilla extract

¼ teaspoon ground cinnamon

INDEX

Recipes included in the cookbook are in italics.

METRIC CONVERSION CHART

U.S. Measurement	Approximate Metric Liquid Measurement	Approximate Metric Dry Measurement
1 teaspoon	5 ml	—
1 tablespoon or ½ ounce	15 ml	14 g
1 ounce or ⅛ cup	30 ml	29 g
¼ cup or 2 ounces	60 ml	57 g
⅓ cup	80 ml	—
½ cup or 4 ounces	120 ml	113 g
⅔ cup	160 ml	—
¾ cup or 6 ounces	180 ml	—
1 cup or 8 ounces or ½ pint	240 ml	227 g
1½ cups or 12 ounces	350 ml	—
2 cups or 1 pint or 16 ounces	475 ml	454 g
3 cups or 1½ pints	700 ml	—
4 cups or 2 pints or 1 quart	950 ml	—

ABOUT THE
AUTHOR

JOHN WHALEN III has been a passionate and adventurous cook since his teenage years, when he had the privilege of cooking under the tutelage of the acclaimed executive chefs Derek Bissonnette and Jonathan Cartwright at the White Barn Inn in Kennebunk, Maine. He is also the author of *Rubs*, *Paleo Grilling*, and *Prime: The Complete Prime Rib Cookbook*.

ABOUT CIDER MILL PRESS BOOK PUBLISHERS

Good ideas ripen with time. From seed to harvest, Cider Mill Press brings fine reading, information, and entertainment together between the covers of its creatively crafted books. Our Cider Mill bears fruit twice a year, publishing a new crop of titles each spring and fall.

"Where Good Books Are Ready for Press"

Visit us on the Web at
www.cidermillpress.com

or write to us at
PO Box 454
12 Spring St.
Kennebunkport, Maine 04046